THREE BEGUMS

Three Begums

The Women Who Shaped My Life

ZIAUDDIN SARDAR

Ilustrated by
ZAFAR ABBAS MALIK

HURST & COMPANY, LONDON

First published in the United Kingdom in 2025 by
C. Hurst & Co. (Publishers) Ltd.,
New Wing, Somerset House, Strand,
London, WC2R 1LA
© Ziauddin Sardar, 2025

The right of Ziauddin Sardar to be identified as the
author of this publication is asserted by him in
accordance with the Copyright, Designs and Patents
Act, 1988.

A Cataloguing-in-Publication data record for this book
is available from the British Library.

ISBN: 9781805263333

www.hurstpublishers.com

Contents

Before

'Mumsey', I once asked my mother, 'what do you desire most?'

She was sitting on a sofa chair, wearing a green garment with red and white flowery patterns that elegantly covered her head. She looked angelic. I was standing behind her. I wanted her to turn around and look at me, so I could take a photograph. I had asked the question unintentionally just to get her attention. She pretended to ignore me. So I asked again. She turned around slowly to look at me, and I captured her. The photograph graces the wall of my house.

Hamida had just returned from one of her trips to Pakistan. The family had gathered to welcome her back. My closest friend and intellectual companion, Merryl, had come from Merthyr Tydfil to see her. My wife, Saliha, was busy in the kitchen preparing a lavish meal for all. Chicken biryani was usual for such occasions. That day, Saliha was also making lamb korma, *daal* (special request from Merryl) and *shammi kababs*—round, flat meat patties with a number of spices and other ingredients that were one of her specialities. My children were dancing around their grandmother. The eldest, Maha, then seventeen, jumped on her lap. Zaid, thirteen, and Zain, nine, clustered around her. Maha put her arms around her grandmother's neck, and lovingly asked: 'yes, *dadi*. What do you desire most?'

She reflected for a few moments. Then replied in Urdu. '*Mere khoaahish, mere hasrat, mere tamana*'. The three words have the same meaning. But she repeated them for emphasis, and sang them as though they were the first verse of a poem. Even though she spoke reasonably good English, she always talked to the children in Urdu. The children usually replied to her in English. She knew that Merryl also understood a little bit of Urdu, which she had picked up from the family, and by watching countless Bollywood films with us.

'It is my *tamana* that everyone in my family in Pakistan lives in a decent house, and they all have enough money to send their children to school', Hamida said. Then added: 'and afterwards to university'. There was a moment of silence. Hamida continued. 'My sister and her husband in Karachi are very poor. It is my desire that we look after them'. She started naming her relatives one-by-one. Members of extended family in Karachi, Lahore, Islamabad, and Bahawalnagar. Adults, children and, in some cases, children's children. She remembered all of them, including the names of the newly born, and vividly described their circumstances. This went on for some time till Saliha shouted from the kitchen: 'Mumsey wants us to look after *all* of Pakistan'. We laughed. Hamida looked embarrassed.

The children turned it into a game. They formed a circle around Merryl, who they lovingly referred to as 'Meeraal'.

'Meeraal', they chanted, 'what do you want most?' '*Mere khoooaahish*?', Merryl said, struggling to pronounce the word. 'What I want, what I really, really want...', she said mocking the Spice Girls song 'Wannabe', 'is love and peace and goodwill to humankind'. The children were a bit surprised. 'What kind of wish is that?', Zaid asked. Maha added: 'not even the President of America, the most powerful man in the world, can achieve this'. 'Be serious, Meeraal', Zain joined in. 'Tell us your real wish'.

'Ah, American presidents!', Merryl intoned. She was quite an expert on American history and foreign relations. 'American presidents', she said, moving side to side awkwardly as the young one tried to swing on her arm and others forced her to whirl, 'are not renowned for delivering peace in our time. Rather, they deliver wars, one after another'. She paused for breath. 'But there is someone who can get us a bit closer to my wish'. 'Who, who?', the children inquired in unison. 'Your Uncle YB', Merryl replied with a large grin of satisfaction on her face.

'Uncle YB' was Anwar Ibrahim, the renowned Malaysian politician and scholar. Yang Berhormat, or YB for short, is a title of respect used for members of parliament or politicians in ministerial positions, similar to 'Right Honourable'. I had known Anwar for well over two decades. He had joined my intellectual circle, the Ijmalis—beautiful ones who sought to reform Islam from within! When Merryl first visited Malaysia, she fell in love with the country and was deeply inspired by Anwar. So Merryl and I ended up working with Anwar. We advised, researched, developed strategies and schemed—often meeting in the evening and discussing and arguing till late at night—as he climbed up the political ladder. He was then finance minister and deputy prime minister of Malaysia. Ostensibly, it looked as though he would be prime minster within a year. But both Merryl and I had begun to have some doubts.

'What I want, really, really want', Merryl continued, as Zaid and Zain pulled her in different directions, 'is to see Anwar Ibrahim become the prime minister of Malaysia'. '*In sha Allah*'—God willing—Maha said, as though God had already acquiesced. 'What happens next', Zain asked innocently. '*Then*, little person of Plumpley'—her moniker for our household—'your dad and I will make sure that he implements all the schemes we have made, fulfils all the promises he has made, to help the poor, to support the marginalised, to promote inclusiveness, and so many other things we have been talking about for years'. 'Will that', Zaid probed, 'produce love and peace and goodwill to humankind?' 'Well', Merryl replied, as she wrestled him away from her arm, 'it will be a step forward'. 'What happens after that', Zain asked. She laughed. '*After that*, little beasties, it will be all up to you'.

'*Khana*', Saliha shouted from the kitchen. It was an order! Saliha, who had been working at a school for special needs children for some time, did not like her food to get cold. There should be no time between the hand that has finished cooking and the hand that gobbles up the food. The children rushed to the dinner table. There was an established order of things. The first plate to be filled had to be the grandmother's. Maha dished out some biryani, poured some *raita*—plain yogurt with cucumber and fresh coriander—over it, positioned two *shammi kababs* next to the biryani, then covered the rest of the plate with *daal* and *korma*, and placed it in front of Hamida. Then Merryl helped herself, loading an over generous amount of *daal* onto her plate. Kids came next, followed by a tussle between Saliha and me. 'You go first', I would say. 'No. I will take last'. 'No Begum. You go first'. I would start putting food on her plate. She would stop me initially with her hand, and then give me one of her statuary gazes which declared: 'do as I say'. I would comply. She would sit at the head of the table only because it made it easy for her to make frequent visits to the kitchen. Even before the biryani or something else would run out, she would run to bring fresh supplies from the kitchen.

On this occasion, Maha yelled: 'Mum, sit down and eat. We have an important question to ask you'. 'I know, I know', she said as she rolled a little bit of biryani with her right hand, mixed it with *korma*, and elegantly placed it in her mouth. '*Mera armaan, mere arzoo*', she began, using other

Urdu words for desire, 'is to set up my own charity for special needs children'. She paused to take another morsel. 'Yes', she said with some determination, shaking her head, 'this is my *tamana* and that's exactly what I will do when I retire'.

The Begums—Saliha, Merryl, Hamida—were an integral part of my life. Every day of my life was spent in the company of one or the other, two or all three of them. Listening to Hamida's concerns about her extended family, arranging for her to visit Pakistan, learning compassion and forgiveness, as well as the Qur'an, from her. I worked with Merryl, both in Kuala Lumpur and London, to ensure that Anwar realised his ambition and her desire. We fought and argued, while she taught me the value of diversity and inclusiveness. We wrote books on America together, as she drilled me on anthropology, British history and the Indian Ocean World and forced me to read Claude Lévi-Strauss, Gore Vidal and the dreaded Jane Austen in the hope that I would come to love her as much as she did (I still don't care much for 'Aunt Jane' as she use to call her). I looked forward to Saliha's retirement, as she gave me unconditional love and demonstrated the virtues of devotion, modesty, humility and courage. We would count the years together. Only ten years to go. Five more years. 'Two more years and I can start setting up my charity', she would say. The three women shaped my life and infused the faminine in me to make me the man I am.

It was 1996. Our collective lives were about to enter an arduous period. The desires of the three women—their *khoaahish, tamana* and *arzoo*—would remain unfulfilled…

Hamida

1

'Batay. Kaya baat hai'.

There are mothers, and there are universal mothers. The iconic universal mother is portrayed by Renaissance painters, most notably the Madonna and Child paintings of the fifteenth to sixteenth century Italian architect and painter, Raphael. The nineteenth century French Impressionist, Berthe Morisot, idealised motherhood in her painting of a wet nurse attending to her baby daughter. The Victorians venerated mothers as universal caregivers. Then there is of course Mother Nature, the universal creative force, the nurturing power of the very abode of humanity's terrestrial journey.

My mother was a mere mortal. But she represented the most significant relationship in my life. When the Qur'an says, 'in pain did his mother bear him, and in pain did she give him birth' (46:15), I feel as though God is talking about me and my mother. When the Prophet said, again and again, that your mother is most deserving of your company, he was certainly telling me about the most significant relationship in my life. She had the devotion of the Madonna, the unconditional love of a universal caregiver, and nurtured and embraced all those around her just like Mother Earth. I idealised her even though I knew she was not free of faults.

My mother was a traditional Muslim woman who held that men and women were equal. She believed that only God, and no one else, had authority over her. That women could do anything men could do. But she did not believe that women are totally autonomous. Men and women were interlinked, and husband and wives were a unit with shared responsibilities and duties. Women were, most of all, the cornerstone of the family. Her world revolved around her family, not just her own husband and children, but her ever-extending extended family: her brothers and sisters, their children, and the children of their children. Indeed, she loved all children no matter who they were and where they came from. She had an uncontrollable urge to embrace them, to nurse and nourish them, to mother them. She could not bear to see a child cry. She would approach even a stranger's child and ask: '*Batay. Kaya baat hai*'. What is the matter son?

Her real name was Hamida. But no one, except her mother and a couple of elders, called her Hamida. Her younger siblings called her *Appa*, a respectable term for an elder sister. To everyone else, she was 'Mumsey'. Her children, and all our friends, and even her friends of her own age, referred to her as Mumsey. My children alternated between 'Mumsey' and *Dadi* (grandmother).

Motherhood came naturally to her, but she knew it could be hard work requiring creativity.

She had no formal education. But she was not unlettered. She learned to read and write Urdu herself and later learned to speak English. She devoured Urdu literature and spoke and wrote marvellous Urdu. What she lacked in knowledge she made up in memory, inventiveness, resolve and an acute sense of rhythm and rhyme. She memorised a plethora of classical poems and recited them wherever an opportunity presented itself. But not only poems. She had also committed to memory several chapters of the Qur'an and a string of prayers, as well as songs and stories of classical Bollywood films and plots of classical novels and fairy tales. She personified a simple fact: without oral transmission there would be no poetry, no written records.

She knew how to stand her ground. She was determined. Patient. Persistent. Tough-minded. And mostly got her own way. She wanted her children to have what she desired most but could not have: formal education to university level. Her horizons were wide; there was nothing that her children could not achieve. Sometimes, she would be stubborn, even cranky. But her stubbornness paid off in times of struggle. For her struggle was not about wining or strengthening oneself but overcoming the hurdles life placed in front of her. It was a religious and spiritual experience much like the pilgrimage to Mecca; as the word hajj itself denotes, it requires sacrifice and considerable effort. When she became determined to do something, she did it, no matter the personal cost.

Ever ready to make sacrifices, she accepted the necessity of doing things she hated—like leaving her parents, brothers and sisters behind and moving to a country she knew nothing about, entering a different time and place, working on the factory floor. These sacrifices changed her, made her more confident, adventurous, eager to travel.

She was not dependent on others. But she knew that interdependence was necessary and essential for survival. From our parents and elders, we must absorb tradition and culture, learn to appreciate poetry and literature, determine what is and what is not acceptable and discover what parts of ourselves we need to keep to ourselves—hidden. The problems of every individual of the extended family had to be shared, and help and assistance had to be sought from other members. Children had to be taught what she knew, and she had to learn from them what she did not know. She solved the problems of life just like the sweaters, scarfs, gloves, baby booties that she was forever knitting: methodically, one knit at a time, with patience and perseverance, until the whole project was completed. And if things did not work out, she would start all over again; just as when sometimes her sweaters turned out to be too big or too small for the child it was intended for, she would pull the yarn out stitch by stitch, roll it all into small balls and then re-knit the whole sweater. A re-knitted sweater is not perfect. But sometimes it is good enough.

I seldom saw a *hijab* on her head. But there was always a *dupatta*, a long, thin, shawl-like scarf that is popular with Pakistani women, draped around her head and shoulders. She was exceptionally kind. For her, kindness was not simply a transactional activity: she gave, others took. It was a shared experience: she gave selflessly, and both the giver and receiver were enriched. She was very gentle but could be tough on occasions. When she did not like something, she let it be known. I remember so vividly the day a group of Tablighi Jamaat preachers knocked at our door. She was watching a Pakistani television drama with my wife, Saliha. I was there more to support than to watch. She opened the door and invited the bearded men in. As they made themselves comfortable in our living room, she made tea and offered them some biscuits. They started asking us if we knew how to pray and do our ablutions. She listened to them patiently and politely, nodding her head, but saying nothing. Then, they turned around and addressed me directly, ignoring the two women. 'Our women', one of them said, 'have stopped praying, and don't know how to do their ablutions. They have lost all *adab* (etiquette), given up their *hijab*. They just want to go out and wander on the streets. They even want to have careers'. Her face turned red. She got up and instructed me in Urdu: 'get rid of these obnoxious men. They have to learn to be human before they can teach others about Islam'. I threw them out.

When she became the matriarch of the extended family, she ensured that it revolved around her. No decision could be made without her consent. And her consent was not always forthcoming, although children could put their arms around her neck and get her to accept almost anything.

2

Hamida Begum Sardar was officially born in Najibabad, a small town in the Bijnor district in the Indian state of Uttar Pradesh, on 14 May 1936. But my own examination of the family record suggests that the year is wrong. Children in those days were often born at home, with the help of a midwife, and their birth dates were registered much later, sometimes after a number of years. Not surprisingly, the parents sometimes got the day or the month or even the year wrong. The correct year of birth of my mother, according to my calculation, is 1934. Najibabad was built in 1740 by Nawab Najib-ud-Daula, a noted Muslim warrior who served the Moghul Empire and gave the city its name. When he was the grand vizier, the Nawab also built a magnificent fort and a famous Jama Masjid. The Nawab's own magnificent tomb and mausoleum is a major attraction of the city. By the time Hamida was born, the town had lost much of its splendour but not all of its shine. It was still an important trade centre and had a thriving manufacturing industry. It was renowned as a centre for crafts, particularly *refoogari*, the art of darning; the *refoogars* restored priceless Moghul garments, such as Pashminas, silk *kurta pajamas* and cloths made of fine cotton.

She was the second of seven children of Saeed Ahmad Khan and Mukhtar Begum. There was a gap of about two years between each child of the Khan family, and all but one had his or her own nickname: Fareed Ahmed Khan (*Bhai Jan*), Hamida Begum (*Appa*), Rasheed Ahmed Khan (*Bhaya*), Zubaida Begum (Choti Appa), Zahida Begum (Bhinnu), Waheed Ahmed Khan (*Bhai Jee*), and the youngest, Shahid Ahmad Khan, was simply referred to as Shahid! Her mother was a strong and determined woman who kept the family together. Her father studied in Delhi, where he obtained his school certificate (Matric), which during those days was considered a good qualification. The family, from the Khattak tribe of Pathans who migrated from Afghanistan to India a few centuries ago, lived in a small comfortable house. When Saeed Khan joined the British Indian Army and got promoted, the family moved to a spacious bungalow in the Bhopal cantonment.

Bhopal is perhaps one of the greenest cities in India. Rich in forests and wildlife, it is known as the 'city of lakes'. The family lived in Pathan Pura Mohala, which as the name suggests, was largely a Pathan area. Hamida's grandfather, Mohammad Zahoor Khan, was the Inspector of Forests, and lived nearby in his own grand bungalow. Zahoor Khan was quite close to the ruler of Bhopal, Nawab Hameedullah Khan, who was known for his generosity and administrative acumen. The Nawab's eldest daughter, Princess Abida Sultana, was renowned for her bravery and beauty. The Princess was not keen on succeeding her father, gave up her right to the throne and migrated to Pakistan where she joined the foreign service.

Saeed Ahmad's family was quite prosperous. His children had a joyous life, moving between the two bungalows. After school, they went fishing, collected fruits from the abundant trees and explored the hills and forests to their hearts' content. As more children arrived in Bhopal, the family expanded, and questions of education came to the fore. The parents decided to move back to Najibabad where educational facilities were considered to be much better. The sons were admitted to a highly regarded secondary school. The younger daughters went to a local primary, where their maternal aunt was a teacher.

There was one exception. Mukhtar Begum could not always cope with a large family. So, it was decided that Hamida had to stay at home to help her mother. She was very upset but had no choice. She spent all the free time she had from housework learning to read and write herself. The house was full of books, and she read copiously.

One day the children attended the wedding of their aunt, who was also their teacher at school, at the house of their mother's parents. The wedding party, *barrat*, came from

Sherkot, a city known for a fierce battle between the British and the freedom fighters during the 1857 'Indian Rebellion', little more than an hour's drive from Najibabad. The wedding party included a young man called Salahuddin Khan. What happened next is described by Hamida's younger sister, Zubaida:

> We watched the wedding from a balcony. Appa was exceptionally beautiful and stood out in the crowd. When Salahuddin saw my Appa he was stunned. He made inquiries and discovered that she was the elder daughter of Billo Appa, as my mother was known. He asked his mother to approach my parents and ask for her hand. She told him to finish his studies. But Salahuddin was determined. He persuaded his sisters to approach my parents. As Appa was very young, they were not keen. But Salahuddin would not give up. Because his mother was highly educated, well-known and respected in the community, my mother eventually agreed. And Salahuddin married my Appa. He left his family and started living with us in Najibabad.

The marriage certificate is just a fourteen by twelve centimetre piece of paper with Urdu writing. The heading reads: Nikah Ceremony and Witnesses - No 14. There are columns for date (not clear, smudged), names of the groom and bride, dowry (50,000 rupees), two witnesses (someone called Hakim Ilyas Ahmad Khan and Mohammad Siddiq) and the name of the registrar. The wedding photograph, taken on the balcony of the Najibabad bungalow, shows my father dressed in simple *kurta pajama* and my mother in embroidered *shalwar kameez* sitting on a stool. She looks like a young woman of sixteen. She is looking at the cameraman; he seems to be looking at a different cameraman, somewhere over the horizon.

All this happened in the shadow of the partition. The division of the Indian continent into India and Pakistan was a traumatic event, the wounds are still bleeding. The change in political borders also changed countless lives and led to the death of two million people killed in the most horrific manner. But the family was not sure whether to stay in India or move to Pakistan. One decision had been made, however. The eldest son, Fareed, then around seventeen, had to go to Depalpur, a small town on the Pakistani side of the Punjab. He could live with his mother's sister and sit his metric examination there. Education had to be continued, even with chaos all around! Every morning his mother, Mukhtar Begum, would hand him a *tiffen* (lunch box) with a day or two of food and tell him to go and catch a train to Delhi and then to Pakistan. Every evening, he would return. The train to Delhi was too packed. Or the train was attacked. It was too dangerous. Or there was a riot *en route* to the station. But one day he did not return.

The news of attacks and killings of Muslims were swirling around the city. There were riots in Najibabad itself. For weeks the family did not know what had happened to Fareed. They prayed and waited to hear from him.

Eventually, the news came from Depalpur that he had reached there safely, sat his examination and, it turns out, passed it.

At the beginning of 1950, Mukhtar Begum realised that they could not continue to live in India. Life had become too difficult and dangerous, and there was no choice but to leave their beloved city. But Saeed Ahmad was reluctant. He was still in service, and wanted to wait till retirement. But as his wife was not ready to wait, he agreed that she and the children could migrate. On a bitterly cold day in March, mother and the children, along with the newly acquired son-in-law, Salahuddin, made their way to Pakistan. They took a train from Najibabad to Delhi, then Delhi to Lahore. Relieved that they made it safely to Pakistan, they took a bus to Depalpur. Saeed Ahmad took early retirement six months later, collected his pension payment and joined the family.

3

They stayed with Mukhtar Begum's sister. Her husband, Hameedullah Khan, was well established in the city. Salahuddin went to Lahore to look for a job, leaving his wife in Depalpur. Saeed Ahmad had to find some source of income. On the advice of his brother-in-law, he opened a book and stationary shop with his pension pot. Hameedullah appointed himself as the senior partner. The shop was quite successful, but Hameedullah took most of the earnings, giving only a hundred rupees a month to Saeed Ahmad. To make ends meet, the family acquired some cattle and started farming a small plot of land they had claimed. The new life in Pakistan was hard and harsh, with little of the comforts of Najibabad. But worse was yet to come.

Hameedullah came to the shop one day and started abusing his brother-in-law. Soon a crowd gathered around them. To avoid conflict, Saeed Ahmad left the shop and went home. Hameedullah followed, and on arriving at the house ordered Saeed Ahmad, together with the family, to get out. The whole family were literally thrown out on the street.

They searched for a house to rent and acquired one with the help of their neighbours. But within a few months, they were unable to pay their rent. The neighbours advised them to occupy a house left by a Hindu family. They became squatters. The house had been abandoned for three years and was in a very bad shape. It was dark and dingy. Badly ventilated. Infested. There was even a nest of snakes. Mukhtar Begum—who had never succumbed to the odds of life and always maintained her dignity—and Hamida worked hard to make it liveable. But there was only so much one could do. Children got boils all over their bodies. One of Hamida's siblings, Waheed, was left with permanent marks and swellings on his face and body. Saeed Ahmad caught tuberculosis, which would eventually lead to his death. And it was probably here that my mother too was infected with this dreadful bacterium.

And it was here that Hamida had her first child. I was born in October 1951. Three weeks premature.

Life in Depalpur was now unbearable. Saeed Ahmad sent his eldest son, Fareed, to Karachi where, with the help of some relatives, he joined the Pakistan navy and continued his education. As soon as he was allotted a house, he brought his father to Karachi to look after him and start his treatment for tuberculosis. One by one, the family began to shift to Karachi, increasing the burden on Fareed, the sole bread winner. Salahuddin and Hamida, along with their new born, also moved to Karachi. Salahuddin managed to get a job at the post office in Saddar, a prime commercial area of the city. Hamida joined her brother in looking after her father whose health was now rapidly deteriorating. And it now become obvious that Fareed too had tuberculosis. A year or so later, Mukhtar Begum, who never complained throughout her life, gathered the remaining children, got on a train and joined the rest of the family.

Life was still hard. But Karachi, a sea port, was heaven compared to Depalpur. A city full of opportunities. The family was together again. The soothing sea breeze calmed the shattered nerves of the household. Marriages were arranged. Hamida's elder brother, Fareed, got married, and then her younger brother Rasheed was married. Soon afterwards, she had her second child: my sister Huma. We gave her the nickname Munni—wee girl! It was 1954.

While a segment of family settled in Karachi, Hamida's husband, Salahuddin, was restless. We called him Bawaji, meaning respected father or elder, a word that we probably picked up from the thriving Parsee community of Karachi. He had bigger ambitions than working at the post office. He looked for other jobs in Karachi, something that matched his engineering degree from Aligarh University. But he did not succeed. He decided to move to Lahore, where his elder

brother, Zafar Durrani, was a prominent doctor. Bawaji also had literary desires. During his student days in Aligarh, he was a member of the Engineering College Drama Society and took part in a number of plays. In 1947, he played Mirza Ghalib, the celebrated Urdu poet, in a comedy: *Zabardasti Ka Hakim* (Forcibly Hakim), the word for a traditional Islamic doctor. His mother, Ahmadi Begum, was a well-known poet who wrote both in Urdu and Persian. As a president of the All India Women's Association, she was noted for her rousing speeches. Lahore is the literary centre of Pakistan, and Bawaji spent some time exploring his mother's literary heritage. He moved with ease in and out of the literary circles of the city. We lived in a dilapidated house in Sutar Mandi, in the old city, where Hamida's third child, my younger brother Jamal, was born in July 1957. The joy of the new arrival was tempered by the fact that Bawaji was still unable to find suitable employment.

So Bawaji moved again. This time to Montgomery, now known as Sahiwal, about 150 miles from Lahore. Montgomery, sandwiched between the Satlej and Ravi rivers and rich in agriculture, had two distinct advantages. There was a biscuit factory in need of engineers and there was a house for us to live in that belonged to his elder brother. His younger sister, Aisha, a medical doctor, worked in a nearby hospital. Bawaji managed to get a job at the biscuit plant and quickly became a leader of the factory union.

Life in Montgomery seemed like an idyll. Our house was a huge bungalow divided into two. Our half had seven rooms, fanned out in a single floor, and an enormous garden with a number of fruit trees. For security, we acquired a large Alsatian dog. Hamida wasted no time in befriending the neighbours in the other half of the bungalow. The two families were frequently in each other's house, sharing food and books—largely Urdu novels and poetry—in equal measures. Hamida's mother-in-law, Ahmadi Begum, also lived with us. Both Hamida and Ahmadi Begum were addicted to the novels of A. R. Khatun, who flourished during the 1950s. Khatun's novels often came in multiple volumes, always had a strong female protagonist whose name graced the title and vividly depicted the culture and values of Muslim families in Uttar Pradesh as well as the turmoil these families experienced during partition. Both women instantly identified themselves with the characters. After all, they had the same stories.

At the beginning of summer, Bawaji plucked raw mangoes from the trees in our garden. More raw mangoes are bought cheaply from the local farmers. The whole lot were then carefully laid out, one by one, in rows in a designated room in the house. Each row would be covered by a thick layer of cotton wool. As various segments of the mango pile slowly became ripe with an orange-yellow or reddish peel, they were collected in turn and brought out. In the evening, the whole family would sit together and eat huge quantities of mangoes. Bawaji was very protective of his mango room. He called it *paal*—his penthouse, but it was on the ground floor. No one was allowed to go in there. Looking after the mangoes and serving them to the family was his job alone.

One evening, Bawaji returned from work and found the house empty. The children were playing in the garden. He asked: 'where is your mother? Your grandmother?' 'We are waiting for them to call us for dinner', came the reply. Bawaji became concerned. He looked for them all over the house. But they were nowhere to be seen. Hamida was heavily pregnant with her fourth child, and he started to panic. 'Hamida, Hamida', he shouted as he ran in and out of the house. The neighbours heard the commotion and came running. Eventually, someone said: 'have you looked in your mango *paal*'. 'No', he replied, running towards his 'penthouse'. When he opened the door of the mango room, he saw the two women sitting on top of a pile of mangoes. Sweating profusely. They were reading *Chashma*, a three-volume epic novel of partition. By candle light.

The birth of Hamida's second daughter brought great joy to the family. As she was growing, she was passed from mother to father, to grandmother, to aunt, to elder children, to neighbours. Everyone wanted to hold and cuddle her. We gave her the moniker 'Chotti Munni'—little wee girl.

During the second week of April 1959, the family celebrated the end of Ramadan with some fanfare. Amongst the conventional biryani, korma and other traditional Asian food, there was the vermicelli sweet (cooked in milk with various condiments) that is traditionally served on the occasion of Eid. Family and guests enjoyed the food, and then, almost by instinct, also fed a spoon or two, or even three, of vermicelli sweet to Chotti Munni. By the end of the day, she started vomiting. My Aunt Aysha, who was present, immediately examined and medicated her. But she continued to vomit most of the night. By the next morning, she was surrounded by a group of doctors from Aysha's hospital. They could not work out what was wrong with her. The following day she died.

Hamida was devastated. She wept uncontrollably. She would look at a black and white photograph of Chotti Munni and sob. It is the only photo we have of her. It shows her on her death bed, rose petals sprinkled around her. Then, she will incessantly hum a poem:

> Spring is here
> Garden in full bloom.
> I weep for the buds
> That wither away
> Without blooming into flowers.

More bad news came later in the year. Her father, Saeed Ahmad, was moved from Karachi to Bahawalnagar—just ten kilometres from the Indian border where her uncle,

Abdul Raziq Khan, was a noted hakim. His tuberculosis had reached the last stage. Hakim Sahib, as he was known, looked after him for a year. He died towards the end of 1959.

One blow after another. She tried to cope with wave after wave of emotions. She would visit Chotti Munni's grave daily and occasionally take me with her. Aysha was transferred to Lahore, and my grandmother went with her to live with her eldest son. The house was terribly quiet, with sadness and despair all around. She did not say much. But cried often. All she had were tears, only tears.

Outside the house, Pakistan was under martial law. Muhammad Ayub Khan, a military officer who had served as defence and home minister, had seized power in a military coup—the first of quite a few to come! Bawaji was amongst the leaders of a strike at the biscuit factory. The martial law administrators arrested some of his fellow leaders and closed the factory. There was an indication that he could be arrested too. He announced to the family that he would be migrating to England, the mother of all parliaments. Hamida was stunned. 'I have to go', he said. She had nothing to worry about. 'You and the children will join me as soon as I find a job and a place to stay'. He left within weeks.

She was alone in a big house with her three children. She enrolled me, with the help of Aysha, who came down from Lahore frequently to check on us, in a local school. She tried to teach what she knew to Huma and Jamal at home. Sometimes she struggled, but she coped as best she could and never complained. Her only consolation were letters from Bawaji and parcels of books he sent for the children. She loved to see me read. 'You must learn English', she would say. '*Fur fur bolny hay*'—speak it fluently. I struggled with *Black Beauty, Treasure Island* and *Kidnapped*. She would ask me to read it aloud to her. On occasions, she would read extracts from the novel she was currently reading to her children.

It seemed like eternity. But two years later, Bawaji finally arranged for the family to move to London. We took the train to Karachi, where we stayed for a week saying goodbyes to the extended family. Then on a bright sunny day, she huddled her three children—ten, seven and four years old—like a mother hen protecting her chicks, and got on an awful PIA (Pakistan International Airlines) flight to London.

4

The family arrived in London on a cold, wet and dark evening towards the end of 1961. Bawaji had rented a first-floor room in a terraced house on Evering Road, Hackney, from a West Indian couple. Hamida was happy to be united with her husband, but was not particularly pleased with London. She—we all—hated the cold; and the winter of 1961–62 was particularly bad. With months of sub-zero temperatures, they skated on the frozen Thames that year—just as Dickens wrote. And the snow! It piled up everywhere and refused to budge, week after week. We had a small paraffin heater to keep us warm and spent most of the day huddled around it. She made friends with our landlady, who was a big, gregarious black woman. Mrs La Verne taught her a few words of English, and in return Hamida shared recipes with her and, on occasion, furnished her with pots full of *biryani*. Life was miserable, she was not happy but, as usual, kept silent. Bawaji, she would say, is doing his best.

He was desperately looking for better lodging. There was no shortage of appropriate accommodation near us. But they all had one particular condition: 'No Coloured Need Apply'. She did not know what coloured meant, and asked Mrs La Verne. 'Love', Mrs La Verne replied, 'we are not white. White people don't like people like us, from the colonies. They think we smell or something. They're prejudiced against us'. 'Some people', Hamida said, 'are nothing more than invertebrates who wear clothes'. I had never heard the word she used for 'invertebrates', *boda*. It took me sometime to realise what she said.

She became afraid and would not allow her children to go out. But children being children, she had to give in every so often. She would only let them go out when they were covered with layers of sweaters and scarves, which she brought with her from Pakistan, and overcoats and gloves bought in London. Once or twice a week, she would put coconut oil on her children's hair. She had brought a bag full of books and read when the children played outside. She would read the Qur'an (a volume with Urdu translation that came complete with cotton pouch) and thirty *sapras* (the whole volume divided into thirty parts for teaching purposes). Anthologies of poetry—*Diwans*—of Ghalib, Mir (a renowned eighteenth-century Moghul poet), Zafar (the last Moghul Emperor of India) and several volumes of Muhammad Iqbal (the greatest Urdu poet of the twentieth century), including *Bang-i-Dara*. Several Urdu novels, including a number of novels by Zubeda Khatoon (daughter of A. R. Khatoon), *Tauba Tun Nasooh* by Deputy Nazeer Ahmad, a novel about the social status of women set during the Raj, and two historical novels: Sadiq Siddiqui's *Andulus Ka Doo Chant* (Two Moons of Andalucia), about the fall of Andalusia, and Naseem Hijazi's *Akhri Chattan* (The Last Rock), about the fall of Baghdad. And several slim volumes of detective stories by Ibn Safi, which I read.

I recall that one day I came into our room cold and shivering after playing in the snow. She ran her fingers through my hair, melting the frozen coconut oil that had given a sculptured look to my hair. 'I know it's very cold, *baitay*', she said, 'and it could get colder. You will need something to protect yourself from the harsh English winters, something that warms you from the inside and keeps the cold at bay, something that anchors you to your being.' She pulled up a chair and I sat on her lap. 'Urdu poetry is our most cherished inheritance. It will warm you when all around you turns into ice.' With one arm around me, she picked up the aging, well-thumbed copy of *Diwan-e-Mir*. Flicking through the pages, her eyes came to rest on a particular poem. She began to hum, the humming turned into words, the words turned into fire, and I was engulfed:

> Look you: it's emerging from the soul of my heart!
> Where is this smoke coming from?

Eventually, Bawaji secured a ground floor flat nearby in Hilsea Street, around Clapton Pond. It had two rooms and a small passageway that connected the living room and kitchen. The toilet was outside the flat, behind the kitchen. No bathroom. We had to share the bathroom with Mrs Johnson, a widow who lived upstairs. The children shared the front room, while Hamida and Bawaji slept in the back room.

It wasn't ideal. But at least it was bigger than the room at Evering Road. Hamida made instant friends with our neighbour, Jane. Her son, Graham, became my best friend. Bawaji started work at the Ford factory in Dagenham, East London. He would leave early in the morning and try to get home early in the evening to study for accountancy. Right in front of the flat on Hilsea Street was the Millfield Primary School. Huma and Jamal were enrolled there. I went to Brooke House Secondary School, about fifteen minutes' walk from our flat. The children came home for lunch every day. And Hamida spent most of the day turning a cold and dingy flat into a home for her family. In the evening, she would get the copies of the *sapras* out and teach the Qur'an to her children.

But she was not looking well. She ate little and complained about pain in her chest. Both Bawaji and I noticed that she had lost weight. She looked thin, though nonetheless beautiful. After returning from school one day, I persuaded her to see a doctor. He immediately called an ambulance and sent her to Homerton Hospital. The tuberculosis had finally caught up with her. She spent several months in hospital.

When she returned, she wanted to go to Pakistan. She missed her mother and brothers and longed to see them. But we were too poor to afford her airfare. 'Next year', Bawaji said. I wanted to go on a school trip and I asked her for a half-crown (two shillings and six pence). '*Batay*', she said, 'you know we can't afford it'. I got upset. 'Why did you bother giving birth to me', I said bitterly. She slapped me. It was an instinctive and instantaneous reaction. The only time in my life she hit me. When she realised what she had done, she immediately hugged me. We both cried in unison.

The next day, when I came home from school during lunch time, she wasn't there. The lunch for all three children was on the table. I figured she had gone to the local shop. But the same thing happened the day after, and the day after that. A few days later she announced that she had found a job in a factory called Lesney in Lea Valley. They made matchbox toys. The following week I received a half-crown as pocket money, a convention that carried on throughout my teenage years.

She went to work every morning, just before I left for school. And I worried all day. In the late 1960s and most of the 1970s, fascist gangs roamed the streets of Hackney. Black Shirts, they were called, and 'Paki bashing' was the name of the game. I encountered them most days, standing outside my school, shouting: 'we don't want you darkies here', 'Pakis out' and 'we don't want your filth here'. They were mostly young men in their twenties, but some were teenagers and a few even went to my school. They moved in gangs and picked on black and Asian kids. I was caught more than once. It was not unusual for me to come home battered and bruised. Naturally, I feared that my mother would be assaulted sooner or later. She complained regularly about racism on the factory floor. 'Pakistani women working in factories are treated by English male workers in a very familiar or degrading manner', she declared. After school, I would go with Graham, my best friend and neighbour, to the bus stop and together we would escort her back to the house. We were frequently hounded and abused by the Black Shirts but fortunately never attacked. 'I want to ask them what is their problem', Hamida would say. 'No, No, Mumsey', I would reply, 'don't engage with them. Ignore them. Walk straight home.'

One day, Graham and I were waiting at the bus stop for her. As she got off the bus, she noticed a black man standing on the side of the street. He was shouting something. She went straight to him, walking past us.

'What's the matter', she asked him in her broken English. 'Have you been attacked by the Black Shirts?'

I intervened. 'No, Mumsey, no. He is fine. He is preaching'.

'Listen to the Word of God', the black man yelled.

'I do', she replied. 'I read the Qur'an every day. I am teaching it to my children'.

'Accept Jesus', the black man shouted.

'I do, I do', she replied. 'He is a Prophet of God'.

'Accept Jesus, the Son of God'.

'*Astagfirullah*'—May Allah forgive me—she exclaimed. 'God has no children'. Then, almost by instinct, she recited *Surah Al-Ikhlas*, the very short 112th chapter of the Qur'an: 'Say: He is the one God. God the Eternal, the Uncaused Cause of All Being, He begets not neither is He begotten; and there is nothing that could be compared with Him'.

The black preacher looked at her bewildered. She was reciting in Arabic. He ignored her and carried on. 'Jesus died for all our sins. Accept Jesus, and all your sins would be absolved', he roared.

Now, Hamida was really worked up. So she switched to Urdu. 'What *Hazrat Isa* died for my sins? Why would poor Jesus suffer for my sins? Only *I* am responsible and accountable for my sins!'

I dragged her away from the preacher, while keeping an open eye for the Black Shirts. '*Astagfirullah, Astagfirullah*', she kept muttering.

If she couldn't go to Pakistan, then Pakistan must come to her. The household was turned into a microcosm of the subcontinent. She created a social circle of Asian women around her. There was Mrs Mittal, who lived nearby, and her husband also became a close friend of Bawaji. There was Mrs Hassan, who lived a short bus ride away, and some co-workers at her factory. I was given the responsibility of taking the whole group to the Cameo Theatre in Walthamstow or the Scala at Kings Cross to see 'two films on one ticket'. Every Sunday. She would scan the Urdu press—the *Daily Jung* or the weekly *Mashriq*—to see what was on offer. The whole group would then discuss what to see. The latest Dilip Kumar double bill at the Cameo or Guru Datts' *Payisa* once again at the Scala? The decision was seldom easy. She wanted Bawaji to accompany them, but he was always ready with an excuse. So, Mrs Mittal and Mrs Hassan would be consulted. Intense discussion would follow on the merits of the offerings, and minds and positions would change frequently before a consensus was reached. As I have written in my essay 'Dilip Kumar Made Me Do It':

> We would leave for the cinema at around twelve, my mother carrying a bag laden with sandwiches, stuffed *prathas*, drinks and a generous supply of tissues. Sometimes Mrs Mittal, or Mrs Hassan, or both, would be in tow. The long wait for the bus, often in bitterly cold or relentlessly rainy conditions, would be rewarded by an equally long wait to get inside the cinema. I would queue

for the tickets while my mother and our neighbours would eagerly look around for faces they could recognise. They had made numerous friends during these weekly excursions; friends whom they saw only at the cinema and chatted to only during the intervals. I would always return from the ticket office to discover that my mother had bumped into a veritable horde of friends and that they all wanted to sit together. The logistics of finding the appropriate seating pattern in the midst of hundreds of similar networks with identical aspirations would have truly taxed the ability of a beach master at the Normandy landings. The performance started promptly at two o'clock and while my mother and her friends watched the films with rapt attention, most of the men in the audience would participate in each film, expostulating vociferously with hoots or hisses as circumstances demanded. During memorable dance sequences, notably those involving Helen, the participants would hurl money at the screen. And like a throbbing tidal undertow to the film's dialogue and music, and breaking through the hubbub of the audience, would rise and fall the inconsolable heart-wrenching gasps of sobbing women. In the midst of all this I would intersperse avidly watching the film with servicing my mother, Mrs Mittal and Mrs Hassan with a generous supply of tissues to staunch their unending tears. We would leave the cinema somewhere after eight-thirty in the evening, exhausted, emotionally drained but thoroughly entertained.

The visit to the cinema was the first of a four-part story. For Hamida, it was much more than entertainment. It was her connection to the culture and values and to the home that she left behind. Part two began with the narration of the stories of the films she had seen. They had to be communicated in full to Bawaji and the children—including me, even though I had seen the films. She would start telling the story—and she remembered everything, including in some cases large chunks of the dialogue—as soon as she got home. Bawaji was not interested; he would put his hands on his ears and declare: 'I already know. All these films are the same'. But that had no effect on her. She would continue regardless. As the films were around three hours long, the plot required some time to be narrated. So, the retelling would go on for a few days. Once she got the plot out of her chest, we moved to part three. Now, she would start on the songs. The lyrics would be hummed, and considerable care would be used to relay the poetic imagery of the song. The children loved it. Bawaji would pretend he was not interested. Then a particular lyric would catch his attention. 'Wah, wah', he would exclaim. '*Mukarrer, Mukarrer*'— encore! She would repeat the first verse, twice, thrice. Then the second verse, also a couple of times. Bawaji's reaction was almost always the same: 'Umm! The second verse does not do justice to the first'.

I remember a particular film that had a big impact on our household. It was called *Do Badan* (Two Bodies), a big hit in 1966. The plot is a true tear jerker. Poor college student falls in love with a rich woman, but her father is not happy and arranges an accident. The hero loses his eyesight but refuses to have an operation. The heroine is manipulated to marry the person her father chose for her but refuses to live with him. She gets seriously ill. Lovers cry endlessly. He becomes a singer, and his sight is restored. She dies when she sees him. He dies in grief. We saw *Do Badan* at least four times, and each time, my mother and her companions cried as profusely as they did at the first showing. But it is not the plot of *Do Badan* that was really important. It was the songs, written by the great poet Shakeel Badayuni, who was also responsible for the lyrics of classic Bollywood films such as *Mughal-e-Azam* (1960), *Ganga Jumna* (1961) and *Mare Mehboob* (1963)—we saw these films dozens of times. The mesmerising voice of the singer, the celebrated Mohammed Rafi who is perhaps the greatest playback singer of Bollywood, ensured that you could not get the songs out of your head.

When Hamida first sang '*Raha gardishon mein hardam mere ishq ka sitara*' (the star of my love is perpetually in rotation, where rotation signifies total failure), one of many memorable songs from the film, Bawaji was enthralled. Sing it in *taranum* (with rhyme and rhythm) he said. She remembered the whole song, and she sang it for him. Our household was transformed.

Bawaji wrote a *ghazal* that began with the opening verse of the song. He recited it to her with *taranum*—which left much to be desired. Not to be outdone, she followed suit:

> The rotating star of my love
> Has come to a halt.
> Life has taken a turn today
> There is only me and my loneliness
> Since the nightingale left the garden
> I yearn for that drink
> Your memory has returned again
> Like breeze from flowers in the garden.
> Ask those ruined by love
> Have they ever seen the morning star?

Worse: she sang it beautifully. A poetic duel began between the two. Bawaji was not about to be defeated. He gathered his poetically aligned friends for a *mushaira*, poetry recital. They were all asked to write their own poems using the first verse of the song: *Raha gardishon mein hardam*. It was a memorable gathering, and it established a custom.

Mushaira were now held at our house on the last Saturday of every month. Our living room was not very large, but somehow a dozen budding poets squeezed in. Among them was Zeeshan Danish, son of Ehsan Danish, a well-known 'people's poet' of Pakistan. And an estate agent who we called Bukhari Sahib, who was quite an accomplished poet. Danish was a reserved man; his poetry tended to be philosophical in nature, focused largely on the theme of social justice. Bukhari Sahib was plump and rather pompous—I thought he was bit of a crook. He had an entrancing voice and recited his poems, about longing and belonging, in full *taranum*. Hamida said his poems suggest that inside he is a good man; outside no one liked him! Ostensibly, it was Bawaji who presided over these *mushairas*, assisted by his bosom pal, Mr Mittal. But it was Hamida who actually ran the show. She would decide which verse would be used as the opening of the *ghazal*, depending on the most recent films she had seen, which had to be written for each gathering. This was the first *ghazal* that every poet had to recite to establish his credentials as a viable poet. After that he could recite other poems he had written. She would sit at the back and listen. If she liked a poem, she would say 'wah, wah', a number of times and ask for the verse to be repeated—'*muqarer, muqarer*'. If she stayed silent you knew that poet would never be invited again. When her turn came, she would mesmerise the gathering.

Her poems used imagery of the nightingale to symbolise the fervent, suffering lover and gardens to symbolise the world, paradise and the human condition. Sometimes she used the similitude of *nazar*, seeing, and its opposite *tezad*, unable to see:

> Evening arrives, and there is moisture in my eyes
> Today again I see your absence with closed eyes

I need to hold him so I can breathe again
Has dawn stopped? Or dirt in my eyes?
Time has got stuck somewhere
Or is it snow in my eyes?

Where would the stories of garden birds go?
Shunned by the world, where would madwomen go?
Those who never experience spring
Where would these desert dwellers go?
In this world, even your own are strangers
Embraced by yours, where will strangers go?
Where will these stories of life and death go?
The candle is burning, where will the moths go?

Pain in my heart is a good thing
Every beat a memory is a good thing.
Who am I going to complain to?
Complaints stuck in my chest is a good thing.
Those burdened with sorrow
That they pass away is a good thing.

The *mushairas* brought a little bit of the subcontinent to our Hilsea Street home. Along with Hamida's constant reiteration of film narratives, they also set the cultural and intellectual agenda of the household. It was her way of teaching and imparting her culture to her children. Ours was a multicultural household with a constant stream of victors: Muslim, Hindu and occasional Sikhs, Pakistani and Indians. All were welcome. All were equal. And, as in most classical Bollywood films, there was always a mullah hanging around in the background. The film stories were also used to highlight the social and cultural problems of the subcontinent: the inequality, the status and treatment of women, the constant battle between tradition and modernity. Modernity was welcomed by Hamida as long as it did not violate her cherished values. As the standard bearer of these values, she decided what was acceptable and what was not. As a Muslim woman, it was her duty to see that her children had a basic education about Islam and imbibed its notions and values. In return, the children had to give her due regard and respect. After all, as she would frequently remind her brood, did the Prophet not say that 'paradise lies under the feet of the mother'?

In May 1970, Hamida, along with the rest of her family, became naturalised British citizens.

By now, Bawaji had started working in an accounting company. Hamida had changed jobs a number of times. From the matchbox factory she moved to an enterprise called AMS in Ridley Road, E8. And then a couple of years later to Novatron, a company that made scientific instruments. Bawaji's efforts to secure a council place finally paid off in early 1970. So the family moved to the newly built Nightingale Estate, located in the Lower Clapton area of Hackney.

5

The Nightingale Estate was built in 1968, during the era of the 'white heat of technology', initiated by Prime Minister Harold Wilson, by the then Greater London Council. It consisted of six towers, each with twenty-two stories: Rachel Point, Rathbone Point, Farnell Point, Embley Point, Southerland Point and Seaton Point, where we lived. The flat was more spacious than the Hilsea Street abode. It had three rooms, a spacious living room, a nice kitchen and, what we considered a luxury, an indoor toilet. Still, Hamida thought that we had landed into the fire out of the frying of pan. The main problem: we were on the seventeenth floor, and the lifts seldom worked. Still, the family was financially better off. There was no need for her to work anymore. So she quit her job. Her last salary for the year 1973–74 came to £310.94.

Seaton Point also put a full stop to the *mushairas*. Bawaji tried to organise some, but most of the poets who gathered at our place were getting on a bit and chronologically challenged. They didn't fancy coming, or climbing, up to the seventeenth floor. Hamida continued with her poetry. She would write down her poems on pieces of paper and leave them all over the flat. Sometimes she would gather them, along with cuttings of poems from Urdu newspapers, and put them in a folder. Poets need an audience, and Bawaji was not particularly good at listening. When my sister

Huma got married, it turned out that almost everyone in the family of her in-laws carried a potential poet in their bosoms. Indeed, her father-in-law was an accomplished poet. So she would recite her latest poems to them when they came visiting, or when she visited them. But inevitably, her poems, along with the cuttings, would end up in the rubbish bin.

For the first few months, she felt isolated, cooped up on the seventeenth floor of Seaton Point. The great minds who built the estate managed to get the aerodynamics all wrong. The gush of wind between various Points often acquired the force of a category one hurricane. Going out amounted to being carried out with a whirlwind. Even hanging washing out on the balcony was a challenge. Clothing would sometimes fly out and land somewhere on the windswept concrete floor. She would force herself to go down to retrieve the miscreant object. Negotiating the passage between the local shops and various Points to Seaton Point was a hazardous task. And climbing seventeen floors while carrying the weekly shopping was no less arduous. Not surprisingly, she was downright miserable.

Soon she made some new friends. Aunties would turn up as a religious and cultural duty to help keep an eye on her children. Her main concern now was to get her children married. And the aunties planned and schemed with her to get the job done properly and quickly. Of course, they had their own ideas of what constituted proper arrangements.

Their first, and only, success was with Huma, after which Hamida focused on her boys. A trip or two to Pakistan was made for the assignment. Certain things had to be accomplished no matter how many hurdles life throws at you.

There were other visitors too.

I was accompanying her for our weekly shopping one day. We found a group of old ladies huddled together on the ground floor by the lifts. They were afraid to walk out into the open as hurricane winds whistled between the tower blocks. We formed a convoy, held each other's hands and walked to the local shops together. Hamida started talking to some of them, and a bond of friendship soon developed. She invited them for tea, and I often found a pair of senior citizens of Seaton Point sitting in our living room and chatting with her. At about the same time, I became involved with Hackney Citizens Rights. I manned a stall each Saturday morning in Dalton market where I listened to the complaints of old people. In the afternoon, I would go to their homes to help—shaving an old gentleman, doing shopping for an elderly couple or just listening to them telling their wartime stories. Occasionally, I got them out of their houses and brought them home for 'curry', the generic word for all Indian food! Hamida would treat them with great dignity, make lunch or dinner for them and talk to them. Her English had improved by now, but she was still not fluent. I seldom understood what they were talking about, but they talked for hours. There was innate and generous warmth in her friendship with old people.

The old visitors were complemented by the young. During the first half of the 1970s, I was actively involved in Muslim students' organisations. Various meetings were frequently held at our house. Hamida treated the young as she did the old. They may have been my friends, but she saw them as her children. Each individual had to be interrogated about his health, family life, what his parents did, and—most importantly—asking when he would get married. Sometimes, she would suggest someone to one of my friends: 'Mrs Hussain came to see me the other day. She brought her daughter with her. Beautiful girl. She is studying accountancy. I think she will be very good for you'. Her suggestions were mostly, politely, declined. 'Aunty Mumsey! I am too young to marry. Besides I must finish my studies first'.

Social interactions made her life bearable at Seaton Point. But it was obvious that she did not like the place at all. Crime and anti-social behaviour had begun to rise. Pirate radios started to appear. Drug peddlers could be seen around the estate. Getting in and out of the estate was a challenge. Bawaji, who was very good at complaining, complained regularly to the council. His haranguing finally paid off. The family was given another flat, in another newly built, modern estate. But thankfully, this one was a bit more humane.

Nightingale Estate became so irreparably damaged that it had to be demolished. It was shattered in the early 1990s, each tower blown up one by one. Hackney Council replaced the towers with low-rise buildings. But one tower was left untouched, presumably as a monument to high-rise concrete jungles: Seaton Point. It is still there.

6

In 1975, we moved to Amberly Estate, near Maida Vale, an affluent area of West London. It was built in 1972 by the Grant Union Canal, a walking distance from a visitor attraction known as Little Venice. The area was made famous in *The Blue Lamp*, a 1950s police procedural show noted for the first car chase in British film. The villain of the movie, played by the great Dirk Bogarde, lived in the dilapidated Amberley Mews. He is chased by the ever so straight policeman PC Dixon. The film inspired the television series, *Dixon of Dock Green*, which provided us with weekly entertainment in those days.

The family flat was on Downfield Close, one of five blocks in the estate. It was on the ground floor maisonette. You entered into the living room, which led to a large kitchen. Upstairs, there were three rooms—one large, two rather small—with a bathroom on one side and a toilet on the other. Hamida liked it. Bawaji, as usual, found something to complain about. He had lost his job at the accountancy firm and was unemployed. He tried desperately to find another job, but failure after failure made him despondent. For a while he worked as a volunteer at a marriage bureau run by the UK Islamic Mission. It brought some dividends: a potential match was discovered for their son, Jamal. Negotiations followed successfully. Apart from some volunteer work, Bawaji spent most of his days sitting on his special chair in the living room, where he read *The Guardian* from the first to the last page. As the printer's ink from the newspaper would rub off on his white *kurta pyjama*, he would ritualistically lay a plastic sheet on his lap and then spread the newspaper on it. The plastic sheet would be cleaned and carefully folded after the reading was done—which mostly took the whole day—ready for the next date. This is a ritual that I also adopted but without the piece of plastic!

Hamida on the other hand spent no time in developing a new social circle. There were the Nurgis who lived on the first floor of Downfield Close and other families dotted across Amberly Estate. But her best new friend, Surita, lived only a few doors away, with her husband Kumar and their three children. I say *their* children, but Hamida soon adopted them and treated them as though they were *her* children. Surita, a devout Hindu, was much younger than Hamida and called her 'Auntiji'. But the two women behaved as though they were twin sisters, inseparable from each other. There was a constant flow of food from the two houses: if vegetable *biryani* and *keralas* (bitter gourd) went one way, *bhature* and *chole* came the other way. During religious festivals, such as Eid (which marks the end of Ramadan) or Diwali (which honours the triumphant return of Lord Rama, his wife Sita and brother Lakshman, after fourteen years in exile), the two households would merge into one extended family and go wild with food and fireworks.

Her children were now married, a burden had been lifted, and Hamida felt liberated. Huma and Jamal had moved out to start their own families. Ostensibly, I lived with my parents, but actually I was working in Jeddah, at the Hajj Research Centre of King Abdul Aziz University. As a result, our financial situation had improved considerably. So my parents were mostly on their own. At my request, both Hamida and Bawaji went for Hajj in November 1978. After returning from Jeddah, I too decided to move out of Downfield Close. I was newly married with a child. A house was secured, and Saliha, my wife, Maha, my newly born daughter, and I moved to Colindale, North London. It was to become our family home for the coming decades.

Hamida returned from Hajj rejuvenated. It was a formal recognition and elevation of her as the matriarch of the extended family. Now, like a constitutional monarch, her consent was required for any and all issues. Telephone calls came from Pakistan asking her for permission for someone to marry someone, or her counsel for some knotty social or cultural issue. She settled into a regular pattern of travel. A few months in London, then off she went to California to be with her daughter and grandchildren. Back to London for a short period before heading off to Pakistan for three or four months. In Pakistan, she would spend time with the family of each of her relatives in Karachi, Lahore and Bahawalnagar. She would take presents for everyone. Clothes for her sisters, brothers and elder relatives. Toys for the children, who seemed to grow in number year by year.

Meanwhile, Bawaji stayed in London. It was difficult to get him off his favourite chair and away from his cherished newspaper. He had become disillusioned with both Britain and Pakistan. He wanted to be left alone—undisturbed. But when she returned from one of her regular trips to Pakistan, narratives had to be narrated. Just like the accounts of the films she had watched, the tale of each family she had visited had to be told to her own family, but most specifically to Bawaji. She was like a bee who had gathered nectar from flower to flower, and once back in the hive, it had to be turned into honey. The process involved not just relating the situation of each family she had visited—who had married, who had a new born, who had graduated, who had a new job—but also the myriad of problems they faced. The tribulations had to be communicated in fine detail, and their solutions had to be found. It was all too much for Bawaji, who, as I was soon to discover, had his own worries. The marriages and inter-family feuds were left for her to solve. Children and grandchildren pooled together to resolve financial concerns.

Bawaji was having severe chest pain that he kept to himself. I learned about it from a telephone call. The voice said: 'your father has asked us to ring you. He is in intensive care after open heart surgery'. I rushed to the hospital. He had walked into the accident and emergency unit without telling anyone. Did not even bother to call an ambulance. He just told his wife that he was going out for a while. Three days later he was moved to another ward. I was waiting as he was wheeled in on a stretcher. As I held his hand, I noticed tears in his eyes. It was first time I had seen him cry. He had suffered so much, yet he remained resilient and never showed any signs of weakness. 'Ziauddin', he quivered, 'I love you *batay*. I am very proud of what you have achieved'.

When Bawaji returned from hospital, I decided that he could not be left alone. By sheer luck, I managed to secure a house right behind mine. With both parents right next to me, I could keep an eye on them, while they would be able to live as independently as they desired. It was easy to persuade Bawaji. But Hamida liked living at Downfield Close and was not keen to move. Besides, she did not want to be separated from her bosom pal, Surita. Undoubtedly, her time at Downfield Close were the happiest decades of her life. Eventually, she gave in to the pressure from her children. The fact that her grandson, Atif, was going to stay with them was an extra bonus. So, towards the end of April 1996, Bawaji and Hamida moved to Colindale.

Almost immediately began the long and protracted Garden Gate Tussle. The two houses are joined in the shape of an upside down and turned L: ⌐. Thus, the two back gardens can easily be connected and one can move easily between the two houses via the commons. Hamida wanted the wall separating the two gardens to be demolished and replaced with a gate so she could come and go between the two houses with relative ease. Saliha was utterly against the idea. It was a classic power and territory dispute focused on our kitchen. 'Mumsey', Saliha alleged, 'will dominate *my* kitchen. She will *always* be there'. This was indeed a natural thing for Hamida to do. Once she entered our house, or indeed any house of any relative, her first instinct was to take over the kitchen. This she saw as her right as the matriarch of the family. Saliha wanted to preserve her independence, and power had to be maintained over the kitchen, the capital of the household. Neither mother-in-law nor the daughter-in-law were willing to budge an inch. Bawaji and I watched the tussle with amazement but remained neutral. There is power in neutrality too!

Then Bawaji made an announcement. He was going to Pakistan. Considering that he was thoroughly disenchanted with the state of the country, we were astonished. He had systematically refused to visit his homeland since he landed in London in 1959. One could detect bitterness in his tone whenever he spoke about Pakistan. We thought hah hah: finally he is homesick! He wanted to go on his own and travelled to Karachi in April 1997, where he was received with considerable fanfare. He visited as many members of the two extended families—his wife's and his own—as he could; and those he could not visit came from different corners of Pakistan to see him.

Meanwhile, the Garden Gate Tussle continued, much like the continuing story of a daily daytime soap opera.

Bawaji returned from Pakistan emotionally drained. It seemed he had aged several years in a few months. He looked unusually slender and hallow-cheeked. He became withdrawn, other worldly and spent most of time praying. His chest pains returned, but he refused to see a doctor. He insisted on returning to Pakistan. This time Hamida was not going to let him go on his own. So, in early November 1999, they both flew to Karachi, where they were joined by my sister, Huma.

On the New Year's Eve 1999, our house was full of relatives, friends and guests. Saliha had prepared a lavish multi-course dinner. At 11.55 pm, five minutes before the twentieth century turned into twenty-first, the phone rang. It was Huma. Her voice was quivering. 'Our beloved father', she said sobbing, 'has passed away'. For several minutes I could not move. I stood motionless. Then it dawned on me: he had gone to Pakistan to die. He had too much fluid in his lungs and found it difficult to breath. The death certificate stated the initial diagnosis as 'marked pulmonary oedema at both lung fields, predominately in left lung', and the cause of death as 'cardiopulmonary arrest'. He was buried the following morning, the first day of the new century, at the Model Colony cemetery in Karachi.

Two months later, Hamida returned to London. She was clearly emotionally distraught, occasionally bursting into tears. I suggested she move in with us. But she refused. I found it difficult to talk to my mother, to say anything really meaningful. But so often, so much is said without saying anything. When I looked at her troubled face one day, I knew what she was thinking, what she wanted. We looked at each other, and she realised that her thirst would be quenched. Suddenly she looked serene and confident.

She had performed the Hajj, but her sisters and the widow of her brother had not. I understood that I had to arrange for them all to travel to Mecca to perform the Hajj, the once in a lifetime duty of all Muslims. This was going to be what Bawaji bequeathed and the best way to honour him. It was done. Just after the first anniversary of Bawaji's death, a *toli*—an assembly of like-minded people—left Karachi for Mecca by sea. It consisted of Hamida's younger sisters, Zubaida and Zahida, their husbands, Abdul Basit Khan and Shafiq ur Rahman, the widow of her elder brother, Monima Begum, and her two sons, Moeed and Hameed. Not included in the *toli* was her younger brother, Waheed. Of mystical tendencies, he was thought to be too unpredictable, too unruly, to be a disciplined member of the *toli*. The young men with the responsibility to look after the elders, declared: 'Waheed Mammu is impossible to control. We can't manage or take care of him. Please don't send him with us'. But somehow, by some numinous enchantment, Uncle Waheed turned up in Mecca. He performed the Hajj with the rest of the family. He was said to be, contrary to his normal behaviour, very disciplined. New stories, even better than the Bollywood ones, were generated to keep Hamida occupied.

After two years living on her own, Hamida finally agreed to move in with us. I remember that day so well. When I went to see her that morning, she was humming an Urdu *ghazal*. I couldn't quite hear her. She raised her voice and started singing in the way she used to do years ago in our— now forgotten—*mushairas*. It was a poem by the celebrated twentieth century Urdu poet, Quateel Shifai, who, like Hamida herself, was born in India, migrated to Pakistan, was forced by circumstance to do menial work and had little formal education:

> On damp autumn nights, elusive tales enfold me. I
>   remember.
> Glimpses of past experience, memories of her youth. I
>   remember.
>
> As buds trembling to unfold, those blossoming lips
> In an idle reverie their words come back to me. I
>   remember.
>
> I had forgotten who left me alone in this world
> When I recall my past, one face emerges. I remember.

Road wearied feet, a few tears, loneliness, the dust of
   travel
Of my lost companion, every single feature I remember.

I, Quateel, the destitute, what have I to say to the world?
Yet in another's strange story, my youth finds its voice,
I remember.

She was what she was because of what she remembered. She remembered frequently and talked animatedly about Bawaji, her mother, her bothers, the mystical adventures of 'Waheed'—she called her younger brother by his name— and other relatives living and departed. But her ability to remember was cruelly seeping away from her.

7

We moved her to a downstairs room in our house. But she occupied the whole residence. Sleeping with her granddaughter or in the guest room when she wanted. And, of course, just as Saliha feared, she dominated the kitchen. The Garden Gate Tussle was now over. There was no real need for a gate between the two houses, but it was duly built anyway. She resumed her travels to Pakistan and California. In May 2005, she went to Pakistan and from there for umrah—the lesser pilgrimage—to Mecca, with her sister Zubaida, Saliha's mother. On her insistence, another *toli* was organised for the umrah in June 2007, consisting of her relatives from Bahawalnagar.

Sometime in 2006, we noticed that she began to jumble her words in English. The syntax was all mixed up. Maha and her brothers would laugh at her mishmash English and joke with her. She would laugh with them. But then, after a few months, she stopped saying anything in English. Worse, her Urdu also started showing signs of strain. I became concerned and took her to our GP.

A few days later, two paramedics arrived to conduct a 'mini-mental state examination'. They asked her a series of questions in English. She replied to all of them in Urdu.

What is the year and date? She gave the right answer.

Where are we? At my son's house.

Say: apple…book…coat. She said it in Urdu.

Begin with a hundred and count backwards. She started and then gave up.

She was shown a pencil and a watch and asked to name them. She did.

Repeat the following: 'No ifs, ands, or buts'. She could not.

She was shown a card and asked to read 'close your eyes'. She did not close her eyes but wrote the sentence in Urdu: 'apni ankheen bund kuro'.

She was asked to write a sentence, and she wrote 'write a sentence' in Urdu: 'ak fiqra likhoo'.

She was asked to copy a design of intersecting pentagons. She was not able to do so.

She was referred to the memory treatment service of our local hospital. I took her there on 1 July 2008. The consultant carried out several tests and wrote in his report:

> Mrs Sardar said that she forgets certain things and was not able to give information. Reports are her memory is getting worse and is more so over the last six months. Further the family has noticed that she has forgotten the English she knew and she is not able to speak in English as before. Mrs Sardar also has difficulty in speaking her own language as she has word finding difficulties. She is functioning self-caring, able to look after herself and is continent. She mobilises independently. She sleeps well and her appetite is adequate. In the morning she feels low and sad, which passes off as the day passes.

'Your mother has dementia in Alzheimer's disease', he told me. I froze at the very mention of the words. 'You have my sympathy', he said. It is not your sympathy I want, I remember murmuring, I want a cure. She was put on Aricept (5 mg) and asked to come back for further tests in two months. I took her back home. The house was empty. Saliha was at work. Zain had gone to the university. She was tired. So I tucked her into bed. Then, I went up to the attic, my place of study and solitude. I wept bitterly. Death is inevitable. But a disease that erases the self, like a pencil portrait violently scrubbed with rubber, is a punishment worse than death.

While she was losing both her language and her memory, she was still very active. She insisted on continuing her travel. So off she went to spend a few months in California with her daughter. Then to Pakistan for a few months. She carried on as though nothing was wrong, and I kept on becoming more and more anxious. In London, at the recommendation of her consultant, she started attending Rosa Freedman Day Centre, a care home for people diagnosed with dementia, one day a week. The care home's bus would come to take her. She would be ready and waiting by the door for its arrival. While it seemed she enjoyed the visit, she also complained 'everyone there is very old'.

Aricept appeared to be working. It was keeping her stable. She was managing herself well.

But her brain was changing, and her body with it. Yet, she had no way of knowing that she was in fact changing. She continued to be what she always was. Someone who just got up, got on a plane and went to see whoever she wanted to see. Every now and then, she would just get up and try to leave the house. She uttered only two sentences in Urdu: '*yeh chala jatha hay, woh chala jata hay*'. This is gone. That is gone. She repeated them constantly, and we had no idea what she meant. Perhaps, she was lamenting the loss of her memory and language. Or the loss of her husband, Bawaji. Or the loss of her brothers. There was a melancholy in the words that was impossible to endure for me. But somehow, my children manged to talk about their grandmother with a frank emotional intelligence that was surprising to me.

One morning I woke up early and noticed that our front door was open. I ran into her room. She was not there. I searched every room and then ran out to the garden. Then ran out and looked around the neighbourhood. There was no sign of her. After over two hours of searching, I returned. By this time, the whole family was awake. And in a state of panic. Saliha started crying. Maha rang the police. 'My grandmother has walked out of the house', she told them. 'Please find her'. An hour or so later, the police rang to say she had been found. A few minutes later, an ambulance arrived. She emerged with a wide grin on her face. The paramedics gave me a copy of their report, dated 12 June 2006: 'patient was found wondering around streets. Patient unable to communicate. Still lives with family'. The following day, two officials from social security came to interview us. We were accused of neglecting her and given three days to replace our front door.

Now she had to be watched all the time. We developed a routine. I would take turns with Zain, my younger son who was attending university and was writing his dissertation, to keep an eye on her. We would make sure she had her breakfast and lunch. Talk to her and engage with her. And Saliha would take over in the evening after she returned from work. We were constantly exhausted. But some relief came when my daughter, Maha, came to live with us. She took over most of the responsibilities for looking after her grandmother during the day.

The system worked for the next four years.

But by the end of 2010, she had lost almost all her language and most of her memory. She would contently repeat two sentences in Urdu—'*ye challa jata hai*' and '*wo challa jata hai*'—this has gone, that has gone. Yet, she still had some capacity for expressing what she desired. And what she desired most was to go and spend some time with her extended family in Pakistan. For the last time. So, on 6 November 2012, my brother, Jamal, travelled with her to Karachi. The first two weeks went well as relatives from near and far came to visit her. But then she became incontinent. She would not let anyone help her, and it became rather difficult for her relatives to look after her. Three weeks later, on 10 January 2013, she had to be brought back to London.

Social services became much more involved now. They tried to persuade us to admit her into a care home. But we wanted to look after her ourselves. We were provided with a special bed for her, along with other supporting systems. Two care workers came to wash and clean, as well as to feed her as she was unable to take food herself. In between, members of the family took it upon themselves to do the necessary tasks. I could not bear to see my mother wilting in front of my eyes. Often, I would sit with her, holding her hand, either motionless with moist eyes, or talk to her and say anything that came to mind to jog her memory.

Sometimes, I would play old Bollywood songs to see if she recognised them. Other times, I would read some poetry. Occasionally, there would be a gleam in her eyes as though something was stirring.

The mental health assessment in July 2014 was devastating. She was exhibiting 'severe global cognitive dysfunction manifesting primarily with confusion, disorientation and deficits in short term memory'. Her verbal communication was nil. She was doubly incontinent and unable to walk. She had 'reduced executing function and poor planning skills' and was 'not able to accurately appraise environmental risks and dangers'. She was 'not verbally hostile or physically aggressive' and showed no signs of 'being unhappy, anxious or frustrated'. I, on the other hand, showed every sign of being unhappy. I saw it as a calamity. My mother was disappearing in front of my eyes. I looked at her longingly: she looked thin but beautiful. There was that smirky smile on her face, almost as though it was frozen.

While we wanted to continue to look after her at home, the social workers advised that she be moved to a care home. I consulted various members of the family. 'It is not the sort of thing we do. We look after our parents ourselves', my sisters said. There was unanimous consensus that we should look after her at home. We struggled and carried on for a few months. But as her condition deteriorated further, the advice became an insistence, and we were left with no choice.

In late 2014, she was moved to Candle Court Care Home, about twenty minutes' drive from our home. The first two weeks were difficult. To reduce her anxieties, we placed a tape recorder by her bed, with CDs of Qur'an recitation and classic Bollywood melodies. The recital and songs worked as comforting balm. There were two caretakers who spoke Hindi. She became attached to them and appeared to settle down. I was convinced that she still had a speck of self-awareness. She liked to have her hair done and appeared to enjoy manicures and pedicures. And, every now and then, she would try to walk out of the Care Home. We took turns to visit her daily—Saliha, Maha and I. We talked to her incessantly and even believed that sometimes she would recognise us. The generous smile and a little gleam in her eyes made us think so!

After a year at Candle Court Care Home, on 25 February 2015, she was given a 'best interest assessment'. A certain Dr Hanif came for the valuation while I was visiting her. In his report, he wrote:

Mrs Sardar was unable to communicate her view to me in any form despite being supported by a nurse who knows her well. She smiled intermittently as I spoke to her. But there is no concrete evidence that she understood what I was saying, who I was nor the purpose of my visit. Her concentration was very short and she got up and left minutes into my discussion with her.

The assessment continued after I brought her back.

Mrs Sardar has dementia which causes her to be disorientated in time place and person. She is totally dependent on carers for all aspects of her care needs. She is able to mobilize independently from one position to another. She is in the habit of walking around so she has the tendency to wander off the care home. Because of this risk she is accommodated at Candle Court Care Home which has key pad code to the doors. Mrs Sardar is neither allowed to know the code nor operate the doors. She therefore relies on the staff to grant her access in and out of the care home. Although Mrs Sardar appeared settled and happy in the care home and has never attempted to leave without staff supervision, she will certainly be prevented from leaving if she attempted to. Although she is not on one-to-one observation, staff are constantly maintaining vigilance over her to ensure that she is safe more so, as she is at risk of falls. She receives one to one staff support with personal care. She has the use of bed roll which is used to prevent her from falling off her bed. These care arrangements amount to deprivation of liberty.

The last sentence shattered my self-control. I started to cry. Dr Hanif tried to console me and then explained that she faced a number of risks—which 'in my opinion justifies deprivation of liberty as a proportionate response'. She was unsteady on her feet, and there was risk of her falling, she faced the risk of dehydration if she was not 'prompted to eat as she has the tendency to forget the food in front of her', and there was even a risk of various forms of 'abuse in the community if she goes out without a staff member with her'. He suggested that I sign a 'deprivation of liberty' form.

I refused. How could I take away the freedom of a mother who gave me all the freedom I have had in my life? Who sacrificed so much to make me the man I am. I resisted for a whole year. But in the end, resistance—as Star Trek's Borg, who assimilated other cultures, often said—was futile. On 25 May 2016, I signed the relevant document, with a trembling hand.

A few months later, we were informed that Candle Court Care Home was closing down. She had to be moved. Fortunately, we found a place for her at the Ashton Lodge Care Centre, which was less than ten minutes' walk from our home. She moved there in February 2017. It was easier for us to visit her more frequently. But by now her condition had deteriorated much further. She was totally immobile, bed ridden, required full body hoist for all transfers, and had been reduced to a skeleton. She spent most of her time sleeping and had to be cajoled to take a pureed diet and thickened fluids. I could not bear to see her in this condition. Worse: a few months after her admission to Ashton Lodge she caught pneumonia.

She was bed ridden, full of sores, and suffering. She had lost all awareness of the self. No way of telling others what she was going through. Dementia erodes memory. Memories are the essence of our being. Her very being was being erased. She had ceased to be, even though she was still alive. On my daily visits, I would sit in front of her. 'Mumsey', 'Mumsey', I would cry out. She would look at me with a blank smile. No one was there. She was no longer a functioning human being. Death, of course, is part of life. We all die—one way or another, sooner or later. But did she, I kept thinking, have to go through such a miserable existence before reaching the final destination? Did she have to lose her self, her essence and being, so completely by the time she is united with her Creator? I would be overwhelmed by emotions and start to weep.

On a bitterly cold night in January 2018, I was woken up by a telephone call from Ashton Lodge. The voice at the other end said: 'Mrs Sardar has taken a turn for the worse. She has been sent to Northwick Park Hospital. I fear she may not survive for long'. We rushed to the hospital as fast as we could. In the emergency ward we were met by a young female doctor. She took us aside to an empty room. 'Hamida is totally dehydrated', she said. 'She has severe hyponatremia'. She paused to see if we understood what she was saying. 'She has an exceptionally high level of sodium in her body'. She paused again, and with her head down, murmured: 'she has 48 hours at the most'. We all simultaneously burst into tears. 'You can stay here as long as you like', she said, and then left.

We tried to console ourselves. I rang my brother who arrived within an hour. I rang my sister in California. Sitting by her side, holding her hands, we counted the hours. Night turned into morning, morning gave way to sunset. We were praying and crying in unison. I thought about making funeral arrangements. But then, by the time my sister arrived two days later, she started to recover. She was in hospital for ten days during which most of the close family stayed with her. The hospital set up an 'end of life care' package for her. Then, she returned to Ashton Lodge.

She remained more or less stable during the next two years. It became harder and harder for me to visit her as I could not get myself to see her in such a condition. My emotions were uncontrollable. So Saliha or one of the children would visit her every day. My sister spent months with us and visited her daily. My brother would often drop in after work. But I would go only when I could muster up enough courage.

Then, the world came to a grinding halt. Time stopped while the clocks kept ticking. And no one could visit her.

8

The first Covid-19 pandemic lockdown in Britain was announced in March 2020. Within a day, shopping malls were deserted, streets were empty and an eerie silence engulfed the country. The lockdown also locked us in our house. Ashton Lodge rang to say no visits were allowed. I spent most of my days in the garden. The air was fresh, birds were singing. I fed the pigeons who were regular visitors to our patch. It was a reminder of how much she enjoyed feeding the birds with me, with a gleam in her eye and that perpetual smirky smile she always displayed, which I had

even captured in a photograph years ago. I would remember her past and start weeping. Sometimes uncontrollably.

We couldn't see her for a number of weeks, although I did manage to get in one day for a few minutes in full personal protective equipment supplied by a kind nurse. She was thin, frail, breathing with difficulty and unable to eat. I felt the deepest anguish imaginable. A few days later, suspicion emerged that some residents at Ashton Lodge had caught Covid. Entry was now strictly prohibited.

On Sunday 26 April 2020, Ashton Lodge rang. The voice at the other end said: 'I am sorry. The doctor has informed me that Mrs Sardar only has few more hours'. 'Can I come and see her', I pleaded. 'I am sorry. No visitors are allowed'. Within an hour my brother, Jamal, was at our home. He refused to take no for an answer. That night he managed to sneak in to the care home and spent a couple of hours with her. She took her last difficult breath while he massaged her head and held her hand.

She remained in Ashton Lodge for three days while we made the funeral arrangements. Saliha and Maha wanted to give her the ritual bath but were not allowed. Only ten people were permitted to attend the funeral, consisting of my family and my brother's family. We had to stand at a safe distance. 'It is so sad to see her go like this', Saliha said, wiping her tears. Under normal circumstances, there would be hundreds of people here from her extensive social circle, she mourned. 'At least her suffering has ended. There is anguish but also a sense of relief'.

As I stood there in wind and rain, watching her being buried, I began to panic. My palms started to sweat profusely. My body started shaking. I was hyperventilating. I wanted to hide my sorrow from my wife and children, my brother and his family. The more I tried to control myself, the more I found it difficult to breathe. For a moment, I thought I was going to black out.

Then I heard her voice. Her words echoing and swirling in my mind. '*Batay. Kaya baat hai*'. What's the matter, son! '*Kyuun parashan ho!*' Why are you worried? And I knew she will always be with me. I will live the rest of my life in her fragrant shadow.

Merryl

1

'Ye, ye. Said Qi. Systi?'

Those fortunate enough to meet Merryl Wyn Davies instantly noticed certain features of her towering personality. She did not have Begum in her name. But she behaved in the defined sense of a Begum: a regal female of stature and influence. She oozed dignity and authority.

She was seldom seen, much like her favourite poet T. S. Eliot, without a cigarette in her hand, and she subscribed to the Oscar Wilde dictum that a cigarette is the most perfect of all the perfect pleasures. She was a habitual forty cigarettes—increased to sixty towards the end of her life—a day person; for her, smoking was an integral part of the very act of thinking and writing, a precursor to a sparkling conversation. And a conversation with Merryl was a noteworthy experience. She would always start with a compliment, move on to small talk, listen with considerable attention and then ask a string of penetrating questions. You would be drawn, by her considerable wit and charm, into an elaborate and meaningful discussion. The conversation could easily lead to her Welsh origins, and the exchange would begin to simmer.

Merryl was born in 1949 in South Wales, more specifically Merthyr Tydfil, which she describes as 'the very hub and centre of the universe'. She was from a family of mixed religious heritage. Her maternal grandfather was Catholic; her maternal grandmother was a Welsh Congregationalist. And they ran away to get married in an Anglican church. Her father, John Haydon Davies, was a hospital administrator, and her mother, Maisey Davies, worked at the local labour exchange (which later became 'Job Centres') as a disablement resettlement officer. Her parents divorced when Merryl was still very young, and she never heard from her father or knew much about him. She and her brother, Peter, were brought up by their mother. Later, Maisey became the director of the Merthyr Tydfil Institute for the Blind and edited the institute's *Talking Newspaper*, often rolling in both Merryl and Peter to write stories for the paper. Merryl was sent to the nearby Cwmbran High School, then located in the sixteenth century Cwmbran Castle, from where she went to University College London to read social anthropology.

She was 'forever Welsh'. 'Wales', as Merryl often said, 'is the land of my fathers', which is also the opening line of the official national anthem. There are hills and mountains and valleys aplenty, along with waterfalls and impressive views. But the local speciality is horizontal rain with a devilish ability to enter up inside one's protective outer garments. It is both, as Tom Jones sings, 'the green green grass of home', and 'wild Wales'. As Merryl explained in one of her columns in *Critical Muslim*:

> Wild or benign in myth and legend as well as real history this land is imbued with particular meaning: *hiraeth,* an untranslatable condition compounded of endless yearning, loving and longing, presence and absence, that underpins one's relationship to home and transmutes it into a moral, even some say 'religious' landscape. To the Welsh our land is always old and little and oh so meaningful because it is history in every sense of the word and this history is an ever-present witness to the belonging of this people to this place. The clouds of witness, all who have gone before, are ever with us and this being Wales they frequently shower and deluge us not only with rain but also with moral judgement.

Her deep sense of history and truly vast range of historical knowledge, as well as her concern for social justice and moral acumen, not to mention her anger at the inequalities she saw all around her, owed a great deal to her Welsh background.

Merthyr Tydfil, Merryl would tell anyone listening, played an important part in the industrial revolution. It was 'the very hub and centre of the universe' because the city was the centre of the world's iron-making industry that propelled the industrial revolution. Merthyr was close to reserves of iron ore, coal, limestone and water, all of which made it the ideal site for iron works. During the eighteenth and nineteenth centuries, Merthyr Tydfil was an engine of innovation: the ground-breaking puddling method for making wrought iron was developed in the city and acquired international acclaim as 'the Welsh method', the famous Pen-y-Darren locomotive that led to steam-powered rail travel was invented in Merthyr and iron and steel from Merthyr was exported throughout the British Empire. The iron works and coal mines were a major source of employment for the city, which also saw a major uprising in 1831 against the exploitative practices and lower wages of workers imposed by iron masters.

The city began to lose its distinction as the world's top 'iron and steel town' towards the end of the nineteenth century, and coals mines began to close in the 1920s. The closure of steel and iron works, as well as well-established collieries, ushered in a rapid decline after the Second World War. Much of Merryl's anger stemmed from the fact that, as she put it, 'Merthyr was left to rot'. From the 1990s onwards, the city has been regarded amongst the worst places to live. Long-term unemployment has remained persistently high, and the city suffers from serious economic disadvantages.

The 'industrial brutalism', as she called it, also left its mark on Merthyr, and Merryl, through other means. She remembered and frequently recalled the fateful day of 21 October 1966. She was seventeen, working on the local newspaper *The Merthyr Express*, before going off to university. 'The day of the Aberfan disaster', she wrote, 'has been, and I presume always will be, alive in my mind. It is the day when one of those naked mountains of spoil turned liquid and rampaged down the mountainside to consume all the houses in its path and the village junior school'. The disaster was caused by the collapse of a colliery spoil tip on a mountain slope above Aberfan, near Merthyr Tydfil. A week of heavy rain caused the slurry to slide downhill and engulf Pantglas Junior School and other buildings, killing 116 children and 28 adults. 'An army of volunteers digging for days where there could be no hope. Their only triumph the heart-rending discovery of little broken bodies'. 'I saw the volunteers digging', Merryl said: 'their look will haunt me all my days'.

Then, there was the aftermath of the Chernobyl nuclear disaster of April 1986, when the northern uplands of Wales began to 'glow in the dark'. 'This remarkable feat of luminescence', Merryl wrote, 'is achieved courtesy of Chernobyl. When the radioactive cloud made its demon passage over the hills of my homeland it met that regular feature of the climate, persistent rain. This enabled large amounts of its devastating debris to make a new home on the hills and valley of my green and pleasant land'. Sheep could no longer graze safely. The livelihood of hundreds of farmers was put in peril. And local butchers, the home-grown gossip had it, had to keep Geiger counters in their shops!

The trials and tribulations of Merthyr Tydfil were written on Merryl's body. But she also imbibed the Welsh tradition of wry black humour for making sure that good cheer in adversity does not let the essence of the issue fade from the mind. She blamed England for the agonies of Merthyr— 'Wales was', after all, 'the first place to be colonised by the English'. And the English had to pay for their uncouth behaviour, cruelty and oppression, and 'foul calumnies'. Despite her overflowing love for Merthyr and all things Welsh, Merryl was not a Welsh nationalist—except when it came to rugby. She was, quite simply, a rugby fanatic; and it was on the rugby field that merciless revenge had to be taken on England and a price extracted for historic injustices. On matters of rugby, she would declare, 'I am Welsh and engage my nationalist loyalties fully!' The Welsh rugby team was 'my boys' who play rugby like angels. When the fifteen fine Welshmen with red jerseys took the field, Merryl became a fuming bull, cheering them full throated, with all the power of her nicotine filled lungs. 'The object of the exercise', she declared,

> is to beat the English. It being a well-known dictum of old Welsh wisdom that the English deserve to be beaten, comprehensively and often. And they always are. As the

saying goes, a Welsh team never loses. The other side only scores more points. Which is a rather profound statement, if you pause to reflect. For what a rugby international does is confirm the identity of a people, its culture and sense of being, this being a nation that has no formal nationhood, just a rugby team to hang on to. They play five times a year and it is that glorious sense of belonging, community, nostalgia and home which triumphs every time. It's a decent kind of nationalism, it may bruise the odd person, dislocate an odd shoulder and dislodge a few teeth but it never killed anyone by design, or sought to dominate anyone beyond putting a few more points on the scoreboard. It uplifts the spirit and leaves one free to be an internationalist, but one who knows where home is, for the rest of the year.

Home was a place she regularly returned to throughout her life. She was an inveterate traveller, and there were numerous other cultures to explore. While still at university, she set out with a group of students and friends to cross the Sahara Desert. It was 1968. The old caravan routes, following a series of reliable wells, circumventing difficult terrain like mountain ranges or sand seas, were still in evidence. The expedition travelled from Morocco and Western Sahara to Mauritania. It was a gruelling and dangerous track. The following year she went to Nigeria where she spent several weeks doing fieldwork. It was during these trips that she developed a passion for collecting, what she called, '*objets*'.

She returns loaded with spears, drums, masks, pottery and many other items of ethnographic variety.

After university, she went back home to join *The Merthyr Express* as a reporter before moving on to the morning radio news programme *Good Morning Wales* at BBC Cymru Wales Radio. A couple of years later, she joined the BBC TV Religious programmes to begin 'a career of anthropology with pay'. She worked on the award-winning documentary series *Everyman*, which explored difficult and moral issues. Merryl also worked on *Heart of the Matter*, a debate series which aired alternatively with *Everyman* and dealt with current ethical and moral controversies. Later, she moved to *Global Report*, which dealt with issues of poverty and underdevelopment in developing countries. All of this involved extensive travel which provided opportunities to acquire ever more '*objets*'.

2

I met Merryl in April 1980 when she was living in Golder's Green, London. I had just moved to nearby Colindale. On the fateful day of our meeting, she was filming an episode of *Heart of the Matter* on Shariah at the London Central Mosque in Regent's Park. The city was going through a tumultuous period. The Iranian embassy was under siege; gunmen had taken twenty-six people hostage, including a couple of my friends. I went to the Mosque both to pick up some news of the siege and to see Zaki Badawi, the Egyptian scholar of Islam and my former colleague from the Hajj Research Centre, who was now the director of the Islamic Cultural Centre and chief imam of the London Central Mosque. I arrived right in the middle of the shoot.

It was not going well. We introduced ourselves to each other. Merryl paused after hearing my name. 'Are you', she said, 'the author of *The Future of Muslim Civilization*?' 'The very same', I confirmed. She appeared excited. 'I have just finished reading it', she said. There was a big beam on her face, suggesting all her problems were over. 'Would you', she said, and paused, 'could you', another long pause, 'possibly', yet another pause, 'sit in the discussion and steer it in a more positive direction?' I was reluctant. 'Muslims', Merryl explained, 'spend a lot of time trying to justify the unjustifiable and end up sounding as if they are defending the indefensible'. I joined the discussion. But Badawi, who I often referred to as 'the luminary', would not allow anyone to shine. My efforts were futile. Merryl and I exchanged our contact details and agreed to be in touch.

A few months later she rang to ask for a favour. Would I help her to convert to Islam? Why would you want to do that? I remember asking her. I have never thought of myself as a *dai*—someone who goes around preaching and inviting people to convert, or as they used to say in those days, and perhaps still do, 'revert'. To invite people to 'all that is good', as the Qur'an says (3:104), you have to be good yourself. And I never saw myself as good in any way.

So, why me, I enquired. Because, Merryl answered, 'I share your vision of Islam as expressed in *The Future of Muslim Civilization*'. Oh God, I murmured to myself, this is going to be rather tiresome—best to disengage. I advised her to think again and forget about it if at all possible. For the first time, and not for the last time, Merryl totally rejected my advice. A couple of weeks later, she went to Regent's Mosque to see Zaki Badawi, who performed the necessary ritual.

Soon afterwards, she became a regular visitor to our house. She loved my wife Saliha's cooking—*daal* was her favourite, 'to die for' she would announce—and we would eat and talk for hours. I discovered, like me, Merryl wasn't particularly strong on rituals. She was brought up on a once a week visit to the chapel, and that was about as much ritual as she could take (although she was big on Christmas). She covered her hair for a few months and then decided wearing the scarf was not for her. She would begin fasting during Ramadan enthusiastically but would lose the resolve half way. We both agreed that the God of Islam was an argumentative God. He wanted us to argue back; that's why He raised questions for us to wrestle with. 'Islam is about finding a way to ask questions', she said. But we also had our differences. I was concerned with the future; she was passionate about history. I was interested in how things change and how we adjust to change. Her interest was diametrically opposite: she was focussed on what does not change, what stays the same, the 'ever present history' and how often history repeats itself. I talked about shifting values; she was insistent on 'enduring values'. The differences became a source of constant tension between us.

Merryl did not like people to ask her why she embraced Islam. But when people insisted, she would answer:

> as a convert to Islam, I have encountered integration. For me it has been a question of integrating Islam within myself (an incomplete process) and myself into the Muslim community. I have never understood Islam requires the abolition of my 'Britishness', or to suggest that the only authentic way to be a Muslim is to become the very model of a Pakistani or Arab. Islam has opened my eyes to the possibilities of living and making sense of the only environment I know, the only one in which I have the opportunity to live Islam: contemporary Britain.

Islam was, for Merryl, all about asking questions: of herself, the Muslim community and the world. It provided her with the framework in which to understand both the questions and try to generate constructive answers. Faith, for her, was a process—a process of self-definition—and 'a schooling in reason'. But to reason requires knowledge, for 'reason does not help unless you know something to reason with'. That is why we need greater knowledge of who we are, where we are heading, where we actually wish to go and the diversity of what we think. She saw herself as 'a fully paid-up member' of the Muslim community. As she stated in an annual community relations lecture at the Kensington and Chelsea Council:

> I, in a sense define part of the diversity that exists within the Muslim community in Britain and worldwide. But one of the other things that I also define is how much I see Islam as belonging here in Britain and being part of the landscape of Britain because what I understand of Islam as a faith is that it calls us to engage with the community where we live. It is the means by which we articulate what is enduring with what is temporal and what is here around us. That is why faith for me is the bedrock of my identity.

We talked endlessly about identity, multiculturalism, the plight of the Muslims, the Western representation of Islam and had heated discussions on the Shariah. She was particularly concerned about the meaning of definitional terms, 'the naming of categories'. When Muslims use contemporary modernist terms, they often say things they do not actually mean or believe. When using traditional language, the terms and concepts of Islamic convention, different people mean different things by using the same language. The overriding example, she asserted, the lodestone for all Muslims, is Shariah. 'In essence, all Islamic discourse today as it ever was is about the meaning of, organisation and operation of Shariah. But the question is what do people mean by Shariah, what does it include, what should it include, how do they wish to see it organised and operated in contemporary terms'. Muslims see Shariah as a systematic view of Islam, as the body of principles, precepts and methodology, she would roar, but what does this mean in the circumstances of the contemporary world?

The contemporary world also made its demands on me. In 1982, I joined London Weekend Television to work as a reporter on *Eastern Eye*—an hour-long fortnightly programme on British Asian issues, broadcast on the newly established Channel 4. Meanwhile, Merryl decided to go on a long trip to the US, travelling coast to coast by National Express. She was exhausted on her return, but that did not stop her from passing on valuable advice. She would watch each episode of *Eastern Eye* with a critical eye and then ring with her suggestions. Don't wear a patterned tie on a checkered shirt, when doing a piece to camera your eyeline should be directed at the bottom of the camera lens, and, for heaven's sake, do something about your hair (I am still working on it). Eventually, she suggested that we should do a few programmes together.

The following year she persuaded the BBC to commission a series of four half-hour shows 'exploring the way Muslims understand their religion'. It examined the key concepts of Islam, such as *tawheed* and *khalifa*, in conversation with noted Muslim scholars. Merryl worked to transform me as best as she could, selected the appropriate shirt and ties for me to wear and forced me to get a haircut under her supervision. The publicity shot for *Encounters with Islam*, which was broadcast in July 1984, is the only photograph of my good self where I look reasonably handsome.

Our next project was *Inside Islam*, a major series of six-hour long shows, to be filmed all over the Muslim world. Merryl travelled extensively researching the series, and we worked furiously on the scripts. Just when we were ready to start filming, the editor who had commissioned the series left for a more lucrative pasture. His replacement had serious issues with me. I did not go to the right university. My accent was not suitable for the BBC. And, most importantly, a series of programmes on Islam could not be written and presented by someone who was himself a Muslim, for he could not be objective enough. The show was cancelled. Merryl was shattered.

She left the BBC soon afterwards. But it wasn't just the cancellation of *Inside Islam* that upset her. She became disillusioned with the BBC when working on *Global Report*, where alternatives to the standard Western development paradigms were never really explored. While working as a researcher on a particular programme, the purpose of which was to take an alternative view of what is development and how it can best be achieved, she found herself at odds with the producer, who was anxious to focus on women's emancipation. She was asked to find a good human story, a girl about to go off to university wrestling with family problems and cultural oppression that amounted to a searing critique of the problem of women in the developing world. 'The only trouble', Merryl wrote,

> we were in Sri Lanka, the first country in the world ever to have a female head of government, where women have always had property rights, where female education is proportionally higher than anywhere else in the Third World and goes on proportionally longer. One can try and tell them that when staying in the village one was treated to long discourses on the problems of the new irrigation scheme, from two large and vociferous ladies while the seven-stone weakling male head of the household said not a word. But in the nearby tourist hotel the oppression of the women was all the rage. And that was the story they filmed. A view of development not so much found in the field as made in western ideas of what development ought to be about.

'The independence of the BBC', Merryl declared,

> is a polite fiction. How can an institution which champions, upholds and extolls and presents the hagiography of the British nation as beloved of the Oxbridge Englishmen ever be seen as intent on espousing ideas and attitudes dedicated to their overthrow? Especially at a time when it is trying to justify its existence to secure an increase of its funding which is set by—you guessed it—the government.
>
> The reality of the polite fiction at the BBC works because the majority of those who work for it are genuine clones, true scions of the Oxbridge English, usually

complete with public school background. Men and women who innately know the language of the raised eyebrow, the vague frown and can follow the gist of an unspoken firm intention without ever needing to ask questions or demand explanation. The whole system works this way, self-censorship hand in hand with understanding the nods and winks of what is and is not quite the done thing.

We decided to set up our own production company: ISF (Informed, Serious, Forward looking) Productions. But we had a hard time obtaining any commissions. Meanwhile, I left *Eastern Eye* to edit *Inquiry*, a monthly magazine of 'events and ideas', supported by Iran. Merryl became a regular contributor and wrote a highly opinionated column called 'Opinion': 'each month, as I write this column, I reflect on the state of the world. Each month I face the inescapable sinking sensation that the world is terminally insane. Each month I state my case, then retire bloodied but unbowed to await the next instalment'.

One particular bloodied instalment came in July 1985. A collection of traditional and, let's say, not-so-traditional, Muslim scholars gathered at East West University in Chicago to discuss 'The Contemporary Relevance of Islam'. As Merryl wrote in a report of the conference, 'the meeting was not an exercise in proving that the contemporary relevance of Islam exists, but a search of ways in which this relevance can be made to work by Muslim intellectuals for the benefit of the *ummah*'. The emphasis was on 'making

Islam the relevant problem-solving method for the complex problems of daily living in the modern world'. The participants were 'invited not to confront each other with meticulously prepared texts but to think aloud together to bring the process of devising a terminology, methodology and programme for action which took Islam as its starting point, frame of reference and intellectual aspiration'. Unfortunately, the loud thinking got off on a wrong foot. Right at the beginning of the proceedings, a distinguished Egyptian scholar from Al-Azhar University, solemnly declared: 'we have no problems. The *ulama* have solved all our problems'. The other traditionalist scholars agreed in unison. Merryl erupted. What followed was a spectacle to behold! The not-so-traditionalists sat back and watched Merryl take on one traditional scholar after another and rendered them speechless. It was as though she was dissecting a corpse with great expertise and equal fury. Who is this fire-breathing dragon lady (a name that stuck), they asked?

After the meeting, some of the participants gathered in my hotel room. They were mostly my friends and regular contributors to *Inquiry*. Apart from Merryl and myself, there was Swedish Pakistani intellectual and linguist Parvez Manzoor, the Canadian Pakistani architect Gulzar Haider and the Pakistani biologist Munawar Ahmad Anees, artist and graphic designer Zafar Malik and the British Pakistani architect the late Ayyub Malik. We collectively agreed that it was our responsibility to liberate Islam from fossilised tradition and religious obscurantism. We were all visibly shivering, not just with rage but also the abundant air-conditioning of my hotel room. We fabricated an initiation ceremony and dubbed ourselves the Ijmalis, the seekers of *ijmal*, the beauty and wholeness within Islam.

After the Chicago fiasco, Merryl started reading widely on traditional Islam. As she suffered from permanent insomnia (thanks, no doubt, to endless cups of black coffee and lavish smoking), her nights were spent reading. She went through my entire stock of Jamaat-e-Islami literature, my extensive collection on Islamic movements, Islamisation of knowledge, and whatever else she could acquire. The more she read, the more she fumed. And she took her anger out on me.

Her fury reached its zenith when she read the works of Abul Ala Maududi, the founder of Jamaat-e-Islami. In particular, his book *Purdah and the Status of Women in Islam*. 'My blood pressure has sky rocketed', she said. I asked her to write an article for *Inquiry* on her thoughts about the book. But she refused. 'It would be unprintable', she declared. Eventually, she wrote a thundering piece comparing Maududi's ideas with that of Iranian scholar and intellectual, Ali Shariati, who she admired. Maududi, she declared, provides us with an all-embracing mechanical answer to all the problems faced by Muslim societies in modern times: 'if only you are sufficiently pious, Islam will prevail and solve all our problems'. She focussed not on *Purdah and the Status of Women in Islam* but on *Birth Control*, where his analysis is based on 'dubious proposition'. As a sociological analysis of Western society, 'he gives us hysteria which is fitted out to masquerade as information by quoting indiscriminately without any context from a variety of sources', even citing 'opponents of control whose position was inspired by the eugenic debate'. 'Uninformed about science and medicine', Maududi peddles, Merryl declares, 'opinionated ignorance'.

She became equally furious when she read Akbar Ahmed's pathetic pamphlet, *Towards Islamic Anthropology: Definition, Dogma and Direction*. She rang to say that it was not just totally devoid of any original thought, but some of the paragraphs in the text seemed to be a bit too familiar. The debate about Islamic anthropology seems to accept all the premises of Western anthropology, she said. From the Islamic perspective, she announced, there are no 'other' societies in the sense of Western anthropology. Moreover, Islamic anthropology cannot be based on a compound of social and cultural reasoning defined by the operation of one particular society as is conventional in Western anthropology. Once again, I asked her to write her criticism for *Inquiry*. She produced two long articles exploring how 'a really alternative discipline' can be developed.

What would that alternative discipline look like? The question was raised at a dinner in Golder's Green, hosted by

Merryl. By now, it had become a convention for a small group of Ijmalis to meet once a month at her flat for dinner and debate. It included Parvez Manzoor, Ayyub Malik, Zafar Malik and myself. Merryl would prepare an elaborate, multi-course meal. Her kitchen would be full of saucepans, trays and plates with cooked and half-cooked food spread randomly across the length and breath. There would be bits of scraps and specks all over her apron, hands and face. On first sight, it looked like a complete mess. But somehow, order emerged out of the clearly visible chaos. One delightful dish arrived after another, and they kept arriving. The conversation—animated, heated, with a considerable amount of screaming and shouting—would start with the starters and continue till early dawn. The discussion on Islamic anthropology was particularly intense. Merryl tried to explain her position in a number of ways; she was questioned and challenged at every step. Finally, exhausted, she declared, 'There is only one thing for me to do: I will write a book so you lot can grasp what I am saying'. It would argue, she said, that there is an urgent need to acquire another way of knowing, another way of understanding the history and complexity of the world we inhabit, a world in which we are increasingly dependent on mutual recognition of our difference and diversity. She asked if I would help. I was only too eager.

And so began our life-long writing collaboration. In May 1986, Merryl sat down to write *Knowing One Another:*

Shaping an Islamic Anthropology. She would deliver weekly dispatches, written on an electric typewriter. I would read carefully, edit, suggest additions and substitutions and return the pile of manuscript. I soon discovered that Merryl wrote as she cooked. Baked and half-baked thoughts and ideas were strewn all over the text. She would change her mind half way through a chapter, spike it and begin all over

again. It was all too painful. But when, after eighteen months of labour, it was complete, and Merryl declared that she was satisfied with the final version, I read the clean, freshly minted copy. And exclaimed: it is a paragon.

Knowing One Another, much like Merryl's personality, is a complex, multi-layered text. Merryl does not think that Islamic anthropology is simply the study of Muslim societies. Rather, it is a comparative, cross-cultural and historical study of all humankind, concerned with all types of human, cultural and social organisation and relations. As it studies human societies from the standpoint of an Islamic conceptual base, it must be a reflexion upon Islam itself. She argues that Islamic anthropology has to be based on concepts, derived from the Qur'an and sharia, such as *adl* (justice), *istislah* (public welfare), *halal* (beneficial), *haram*, (harmful), *ilm* (knowledge) and *fitrah* (the created inherent nature of humanity). Theory building should begin with an understanding of *fitrah*, which is unitary and the same for all humankind; it is moral nature, has passion and reason and the capacity and capability to apprehend both the seen and the unseen. This is emphasised in the famous Qur'anic verse, 'We have created you male and female and have made you nations and tribes that you may know one another' (49:13); the study of societies and cultures, from an Islamic perspective, is essentially a commentary on, and an attempt to understand, this verse in the contemporary world. The concepts of Islam function as a system, she asserts, but not as a system with a definitive concrete form. Islam is not culturally specific, and, as the verse indicates, it recognises the validity of diverse social and cultural forms which are themselves ways of knowing. Islam, Merryl argues, is a system of 'permissible structures' that emphasise the plasticity of human nature and society in achieving normative ends by diverse forms and means. Studying other societies therefore actually extends our understanding of the potential meaning of Islamic concepts and ways in which this understanding can be applied to ordering, planning and determining the course of society in the future. Islamic anthropology therefore is not seeking merely to record diversity, or even to understand the nature of diversity. Rather, it is a study seeking to penetrate through the diversity of form demonstrated by different societies and cultures to apprehend the consonance of normative behaviour. Merryl does not call her approach to understanding societies and culture 'Islamic anthropology' or 'Islamic sociology'. She calls her enquiry, after ibn Khaldun, *Ilm ul Umran*: knowledge of human aggregation which is the organised habitation (*umran*) of the world. *Ilm ul Umran,* she asserts, carries a greater significance, a clear indication of relevant questions and is a better basis for both discourse and dialogue than is the unqualified label 'Islamic anthropology'. When the name of the discipline changes to *Ilm ul Umran,* it signifies that an entire system of Islamic thought is necessary to carry it forward; thus, it can never be an appendage to the dominant Western discipline.

The following year, Merryl and I went to Kuala Lumpur to work on an issue of *Inquiry* devoted to Malaysia. She made a beeline to Dewan Bahasa dan Pustaka, the national Language and Literature Development Agency, and interviewed a number of writers—including the noted novelist Samad Ismail, short story writer Kris Mas, the literary superstar A. Samad Said and spent time 'listening to poems of love, sweet melodies from the Garden of Grace' by the poet Kemala. I took the opportunity to reconnect with my friend, Malaysian politician and intellectual, Anwar Ibrahim. We spent some time discussing issues of tradition and modernity, the problems of the Islamic movement, the lack of critical thought in Muslim circles and the then hot topic 'Islamisation of knowledge'. I suggested Anwar join the Ijmalis; he proposed that the Ijmalis should organise a series of 'intellectual discourses' to introduce their ideas and thoughts to Malaysian academics, thinkers and writers. Both suggestions were met with approval. The *Inquiry* issue on Malaysia, with Merryl's article on Malaysian writers, was published in September 1987. But a month before, I was summarily dismissed from *Inquiry* for writing an unfavourable review of a mediocre book by an Iranian scholar (*Inquiry* closed soon afterwards). So, we found ourselves heading east.

3

We organised a string of 'intellectual discourses' in Malaysia, anything from short seminars at universities to full-fledged three-day conferences. Topics ranged from contemporary Western thought to criticism of 'Islamisation of knowledge' to 'the futures of the *ummah*'. There was a memorable three-day 'visioning' workshop where we tried to persuade scholars from the International Islamic University Malaysia to imagine a future Muslim society with totally reformed and reformulated Shariah but failed. For the Ijmalis, it was all cerebrally exciting, considerable fun, quite exhausting and sometimes very frustrating.

But Merryl's attentions were elsewhere. She wanted to get back to television. And there was a newly established television channel, TV3, which offered opportunities. With Anwar's help, ISF Productions got its first commission: *Faces of Islam*, a twelve-part, half-hour discussion programme that examined contemporary problems and issues in terms of twelve Islamic concepts: *din, tawhid, kitab, sirah, sharia, adil, ibadah, ilm, khalifa, dawa, jihad* and *ummah*. We gathered some of the most original thinkers, writers and activists—from as far away as Pakistan and Nigeria, Saudi Arabia and Malaysia, Sudan and Turkey, and Australia and Canada—and asked how their chosen concept applied to the problems of the modern world. After the broadcast of *Faces of Islam*, Merryl and I became consultants for TV3.

In 1988, Merryl moved to Kuala Lumpur, and I began commuting between London and there. We rented an apartment in Menarah Indah in the Taman TAR neighbourhood, opposite Kelab Darul Ehsan, a golf and recreation club. Apart from working at TV3, we became advisors to Anwar, with added responsibilities for Merryl of writing his speeches. At TV3, our job was to bring some professionalism into the station's newsroom, train their broadcast journalists and presenters and create some new programmes. We established the *Seven O'Clock News*, launched a business show, *Money Matters*, and tried to introduce as much objectivity into TV3's coverage as possible.

It was not an easy task. We found it difficult to get the journalists not to rely too much on press releases and government handouts. To write scripts to pictures. To even shoot sequences. I would often throw my hands in the air and give up. But Merryl persisted. She would spend hours in the newsroom rewriting scripts and coaching producers, hours in the studio directing and training newsreaders and presenters. She would work way past midnight, return to Menarah Indah for a couple of hours of sleep and be back at TV3 before dawn. We had to constantly critique the stories that were being shot and produced, and we had to do it without anyone getting upset or demoralised, and—this is very important in Malaysia—'losing face'.

So, we developed our own language to deal with the situation. It was a mixture of words taken from English, Malay, Chinese and other languages, jumbled together to sound like gibberish. Indeed, to outsiders it was claptrap, but for us it was patent precision. Part serious, part play, it was also a reflection of our special bond. '*Ye, ye*' was both our 'Hello!' and an indication that what follows is code. '*Said Qi*': what does Qi, the vital force of every living entity in Chinese culture (which we pronounced as ki), have to say? In other words, what is your assessment of a particular piece—a news story that has just been shot, or a particular script you have seen? The Malay word for system is simply *system*; we corrupted it to *systi*, which could have different meanings in different contexts. In the TV3 context, it meant does it work—does the news report have enough substance to be broadcast? '*No systi*', meant it was rubbish and had to be ditched. '*Little systi*' suggested it required lots of work from us to bring it up to a professional standard. Or, as Merryl would announce triumphantly: '*we have systi*'.

We discovered that our language worked equally well when it came to dealing with Anwar and his staff. In certain meetings, we could not always express our frank opinion openly or disagree with each other in front of others. Coded communication between us brought us both to the same page. When we were asked to undertake a task, and Merryl was not sure if I actually wanted to do it, she would say: '*systi possible?*' I would reply: '*can be had*'. Alternatively: '*not *maujood'*—*maujood* being the Arabic word for existing or present. Other terms were added to our lingo, bits from Urdu and French, and it became quite a concoction. Pretty soon, what was meant to be limited to the TV3 newsroom, became, to the utter bewilderment of others, our common mode of communication.

This was the happiest period of Merryl's life, and by now she had become an integral part of my life. She was doing all that she loved: working for television, engaging in intellectual pursuits and heated cerebral discussions, helping to shape policies she believed in and when the time permitted, doing occasional pieces of serious writing. She was the godmother of my three children, a role she took very seriously. They grew up under her shadow and became very close to her. She referred to my house as 'Plumpley', ye olde English name for a village in Cheshire meaning both plum and plum tree but also signifying creativity, curiosity, charm, friendliness, cheer and social life. On every birthday of every child, she sent a special birthday fax, sometimes written in our prattle, sometimes in her own equally barmy patois. An example of a birthday greeting sent to my son, Zaid:

We Prevail!
As we forewarned, we are now EPIC, a universal
blockbuster nonpareil.

As was to be expected the world now beats a path to
Plumpley, lavishing us with their monetary wares and
seeking what they can of our goods and services (chattels
not included, batteries not needed).
Yet we the EPIC of Plumpley still remember from our
humbler more modest days that this is
A DAY TO REMEMBER
A day when our esteemed free citizen moves ever onward
chronologically
with grace and style included at no extra charge (as
defined by the Plumpley Ministry of Financial
Accounting and Crediting and usable for tax purposes).
HAPPY BIRTHDAY
NOBLE FREE CITIZEN OF PLUMPLEY

One particularly intellectual pursuit took her to Mecca. I
was involved in organising an International Islamic
Conference entitled, 'Da'wa and Development of Muslim
World: The Future Perspective'. Organised by the Jeddah-
based Muslim World League, it was held on 11–15 October
1987 with the participation of over 200 delegates from all
over the world. The objective of the conference was to
rethink the notion of *dawa* and broaden its scope from
preaching about Islam. 'Our objective', the conference
prospectus stated, 'is a course of *dawa* that tackles hunger,
illiteracy, unemployment, poverty and the need for a secure
and better future according to the concepts and values of
Islam'. We had worked out a very detailed outline of the

subjects that the Conference was to cover, ranging from living environment to economic and financial development, education and human resources, managing law and order, science, technology and information, media and literature. Merryl was the only single female delegate at the conference.

She had to travel to Mecca on her own. An undertaking not permitted by the laws of the Kingdom, which required all women to be accompanied by their 'guardian'. We thus had to acquire special permission to be allowed into Saudi Arabia without a male chaperone. It was a letter from the King himself—Fahd bin Abdulaziz Al Saud. Merryl arrived two days before the conference, all covered up and looking like, as our friend Zafar Malik said, 'a kamikaze pilot'. She became the second woman to travel to Mecca on her own in recent history (the first was Lady Evelyn Cobbold who arrived in Mecca on 26 March 1933 as a personal guest of King Abdul Aziz). She was met by the protocol officers who took her straight to Mecca Intercontinental, then located on the outskirts of the city, where the conference was being held. On arriving at the hotel, she insisted on going immediately to the *haram*—to visit the Kaaba in the Sacred Mosque. I was busy with conference matters and asked Zafar to take her. She entered the *haram*, stood in front of the Kaaba for a few moments and then fell to her knees. 'She sobbed uncontrollably', Zafar said. She spent considerable time praying and crying.

Much to her annoyance, Merryl was confined to the women's quarters. But she wasted no time in taking charge of the group, a mixture of female scholars, scientists and thinkers and wives of delegates, and began to, as one Saudi official said, 'mislead' them. She became a centre of attention not just among female participants but also among Saudi delegates and officials. She received a number of unsavoury calls in the middle of the night. We made formal complaints to no effect. But not all the calls were unpleasant. She received a number of proposals for marriage. All of which she rejected out of hand—except one. She consulted with me about it. It came from Abdo Yamani.

Yamani, a short portly man, was a highly respected figure and well-known philanthropist. A native of Mecca, he went to Cornell University to study geology and taught at various Saudi universities before becoming the minister of information. He was also an accomplished writer with a string of books, on Islam and cultural issues, to his name. During that time, he was chairman of Dallah Al-Baraka, a Saudi multinational company established by Saleh Kamal, the founder of al-Baraka bank, who had partly funded the Mecca conference. Merryl asked me what I thought of Abdo Yamani. I recalled an incident when Yamani found himself alone in London and called me to take him out to dinner. On our walk from his hotel to a *halal* restaurant (he was insistent that it should be a certified *halal* eatery!), we came across a homeless man. Yamani stopped in front of the man.

He was clearly moved by the plight of the man. He took out his wallet and handed it to him. I ended up paying for the dinner! He was, I said, the kind of Saudi (more precisely, Hijazi) one could love and respect. They say, when you can't find anyone to support a humanitarian project, you go to Abdo Yamani. And, I added for good measure, as far as humanitarian projects go, you are up there on the top of the list. Think of all the *objets* you can acquire! Merryl gave serious thought to the proposal, mulling it over for a couple of days. Finally, she decided against it. 'I can't bear to live in Saudi Arabia', she said.

The conference was a disaster. But we managed to get three books out of it. I collected a pile of papers on *dawa*, community, refugees and communication and sent it to her with a note: 'here is a *buku* what you have writted'. She edited the papers meticulously and turned it into a book, which she called *Beyond Frontiers: Islam and Contemporary Needs*.

While we were still working on the books of the Mecca conference, another book was published that would have a major impact on our lives: *The Satanic Verses* by Salman Rushdie. Both of us read the novel, and both of us were equally upset and angry. The Muslim community had few academics and intellectuals to defend its position, and it was not always defended in the best possible way. The situation became worse after the 14 February 1989 fatwa by Ayatollah Khomeini. We found the undiluted racism and

Islamophobia that emerged, often in the guise of liberalism and freedom of expression, deeply disturbing. It repeatedly reduced Merryl to tears; on a number of occasions, she cried for days. I wrote a few columns for the newspapers and appeared on some television programmes to defend our corner. But that was not enough. We had to do something much more. Rushdie's novel needed a proper knowledgeable response. One evening in Kuala Lumpur, a meeting was held with Anwar in his study. We discussed the novel and our potential responses till late at night. It was finally decided that, in the best tradition of Islamic intellectual history, a book should reply to a book. It was going to be a serious task that could not be undertaken in our little Menarah Indah apartment. Anwar agreed that Merryl should go back to London and stay there until the book was written. So, in March 1989, Merryl returned home to Merthyr and sat down to write *Distorted Imagination: Lessons from the Rushdie Affair*.

We knew exactly what we had to say and write. Merryl would raise questions, I would try and explore the questions, and it would become the first draft, or part, of a chapter. It would go to Merryl who would expand, add further arguments, analysis and examples, and it came back to me for a final polish. We had each bought ourselves an Apricot laptop computer: it was rather heavy, ran MS-DOS, had an orange screen, (what we considered then to be) a massive 20 Mb of memory and was the first computer to use 3.5 inch floppy disks, rather than the 5.25 inch disks which were the norm at the time. Our word processor was called Wordcraft 2.00, which was easy to use but also full of sophisticated features (the best word processor I have ever used). Envelopes stuffed with floppy disks flew between London and Merthyr. When we finished the book, it was stored on 14 floppy disks. It took well over a year, during which we experienced what I can now call my first lockdown. I did not go out for days, and for days I resembled a mullah with an uncouth beard. Merryl gained several pounds in weight. When *Distorted Imagination* was finally published, Anwar declared it to be a 'masterpiece'.

4

Merryl returned to Kuala Lumpur in March 1991, a week before Anwar became minister of finance. She had complained that our apartment in Menarah Indah was too small; it was cluttered with our books, and there was hardly any space to move. So, we moved to a new villa in Section 17, Petaling Jaya. Our TV3 commitments were reduced, and Merryl had a bit more time to travel. She went to Thailand, Cambodia, India and New Zealand to meet Muslim communities, give a few lectures and, of course, collect *objets*. She turned one room into a video library, with a sophisticated air-conditioning system that was needed to maintain the videos in prime condition in the unforgiving heat of Kuala Lumpur. It contained Hollywood output going back to the silent film era, British movies and television series, as well as classics of Japanese, Iranian and Indian cinema—hundreds of videos, legal and pirated. An area was devoted to displays of her *objet* collection. I was barred from this part of the house. 'Chappu', she declared, 'you are too clumsy and too prone to breaking things'.

She began to describe Kuala Lumpur as her second home, but not secondary! She loved the place. The people. Everything about it. If I were to criticise any aspect of Malay culture, or the conspicuous absence of intellectual thought in the archipelago, she would pounce on me. In her presence, barefaced criticism of Malays and their culture, customs, history or food could not be tolerated. She made frequent trips to Malacca, compulsively collected books and artefacts on the history of Southeast Asia and became obsessive over the 'Indian Ocean World'. We agreed on demarcation and did our work in our designated areas. Or, at least that was the arrangement.

It was a particularly creative period in our lives. Merryl decided to write a history of Islam from the perspective of the Indian Ocean World. I had to write an essay on Bollywood and its impact on the British Asian community for a book on Indian cinema that my friend, the Indian intellectual and cultural theorist, Ashis Nandy, was editing. I had also decided to write a critical evaluation of postmodernism. Merryl seemed more interested in what I was doing rather than her own book. She was, as Anwar has noted, 'a cinephile without equal'. She would talk about films with Anwar at great length—not just about classic Hollywood films they had seen, but to my surprise, also Bollywood movies and films of the great Malaysian director, writer and actor, P. Ramlee (1929–73). I had to study a few selected classics of Bollywood—films of Dilip Kumar, Guru Dutt and Amitabh Bachchan. We watched these films together as I took notes. I suspected that Merryl could not follow them as they had no subtitles. When I started writing the essay, she would come and stand behind me—and laugh loudly. 'Don't you know anything about your own culture?', she would shout. And then proceed to present an analysis that would undermine all that I was saying in the essay. 'Am I writing *this*, or are you?', I would shout back. 'You should only write about things you know something about', she would exclaim. We fought constantly, and what I thought would be a relatively easy essay to write turned into a mega enterprise.

I abandoned all notions of writing while I was in Kuala Lumpur. I would do most of my writing in my attic in London. But Merryl's video collection was a treasure trove, and her insights into film incredibly valuable. Indeed, her collection of books, videos and artefacts had become so large that it became necessary for us to move to a larger premises. When Anwar became deputy prime minister in December 1993, the time was as right as any for a move to a bigger villa in another section of Petaling Jaya. More *objets* were secured, and the villa began to resemble an anthropological museum.

When I mentioned that I was thinking of beginning my next book, *Postmodernism and the Other*, with an analysis of the British television series *The Prisoner* (1967), she told me not to write a word till she had her say. I considered *The Prisoner*, about a secret agent who suddenly resigned and is then imprisoned in a shadowy village from where he constantly tries to escape, to be the first authentic postmodern product. Merryl had all the seventeen episodes in her library. She was an active member of St. David's Society, the organisation of the Welsh expatriates in Kuala Lumpur. Members of the society were invited to 'The Prisoner Weekends' during which the gathering watched three or four episodes, and Merryl regaled all, animatedly and loudly and accompanied with abundant 'food and beverage', with her take on what *The Prisoner* was all about, and the coded messages in each episode.

Meanwhile, her own project was quasi static. Whenever she interfered with my writing, I would simply yell: 'Indian Ocean World'. She would retire with a huff. It became shorthand for infuriating her. I must confess, for the sake of truth, that I took some delight in annoying her. It was often when she was fully charged up that she came out with *bon mots*.

She got as far as writing the introduction. Merryl argued that the trading world of the Indian Ocean predates the coming of Islam. It was certainly established by the first century when Indianised states emerged across Southeast Asia from the Champa states on the coast of Vietnam, to Funan in modern Thailand, and across the Indonesian archipelago, principally on Java, where the states of Majapahit and Sri Vijaya arose and held territory on many islands as well as the Malaysian peninsula. 'Arab seamen and traders were part of this trading world', she wrote,

as details of the life of Prophet Muhammad indicate. It is these long-established trading connections borne on the monsoon winds that produced the gradual spread of Islam throughout the region. The Malay world, the islands of Indonesia and peninsula Malaysia, were the place where the various branches of this extensive trading world met. Traders came in search not only of spices but also tin, precious metals and the other produce of this rich and varied region. The Indianised states of Majapahit and Sri Vijaya on Java had been centres of Hindu and Buddhist learning long before the coming of Islam. The regular monsoon winds that brought traders to this region meant they had to remain for a period of months before the change in wind direction enabled them to make their return home. It is through this pattern of regular often extended interaction that Muslim traders and travellers introduced Islam to the Malays. By 1000 Muslim trading ports begin to emerge and by 1200 a Malay Muslim state was in existence in Acheh on the northern tip of the island of Sumatra. A succession of Muslim Malay states rose to prominence in succeeding centuries. They grew through the facilities they provided traders, and their own participation in regional trade, extended their control over territory that straddled various islands and parts of peninsula Malaysia and then declined when tensions between the port city and its hinterland caused internal disruption. Another port would then begin its rise to prominence as the focus of a new state. The last great trading centre to arise was Melaka, on the Malay peninsula, a Malay Muslim state with a Malay speaking Chinese population and numerous groups of Indian traders both Muslim and Hindu. It was, according to the Portuguese writer Thomas Pires 'the emporium of all the world.' So important was Melaka that capturing the city was a major objective of the Portuguese invaders of the Indian Ocean, with whom Pires travelled and whose history he wrote. The Melaka Sultanate fell to the Portuguese in 1511. The remnants of the sultanate removed to Jahore where they established a new state. The coming of Europe imposed new constraints on the whole Indian Ocean, but Malay states continued to exist, to develop the resources of their environment that made them such a lure for colonial expropriation on a more systematic basis in later centuries.

The trading world of the Indian Ocean, she argued, was the first period in history of true globalisation.

The East coast of Africa was an integral part of the Indian
Ocean trading world. In the lifetime of Prophet
Muhammad, we saw that there was abundant contact
between Arabia and the Horn of Africa. The Yemen had
from the earliest times been connected to the region of
Somalia, just as the Nile had connected Egypt to the Sudan
since Pharonic times. Both of these ancient connections
provided the means for Islam to spread organically through
East Africa. After 900 Islam began to spread down the
eastern coast of the continent into the region referred to as
al-Zanj. It led to the establishment of a series of black
African states in the coastal regions of Kenya, Tanzania—
the name derived from the fusion of Tanganikya with the
Muslim Island of Zanibar—as far south as Sofala in
modern Mozambique. These coastal trading states were in
contact with the interior of Africa from which they
acquired such products as gold, ivory and slaves and to
which they traded the produce of the whole Indian Ocean
trading world. Chinese pottery is among the artefacts that
have been excavated at the site of Great Zimbabwe, the
stone city in the heart of the modern nation to which it
gave its name. The Muslim culture of coastal East Africa
was part of the wider ambit of Muslim civilization. When
Vasco da Gama made the initial European entry into the
Indian Ocean in 1498 after nearly a century of Portuguese
exploration around the coast of Africa his objective was to
reach India. In the port of Malindi, in modern Kenya, he
hired a Muslim pilot used to travelling this familiar route
who guided him to Calicut. Some sources suggest the pilot

was ibn Majid, a native of East Africa who was a leading authority on geography and author of some 14 books on the subject. This is most probably an apocryphal tale, but its strong irony conveys a reality European history has expunged. European expansion, seen as an epic heroic endeavour undertaken in the spirit of scientific inquiry did no more than stumble into an existing, long established and highly sophisticated world whose connective tissue was Muslim civilization.

She couldn't concentrate on her own writing because her mind was elsewhere. The fact that Anwar was deputy prime minister was not necessarily a good thing, Merryl thought, particularly under a rather controlling and increasingly cantankerous prime minister, Mahathir Mohamad. The fact that he was also overseeing the anti-corruption agency was even more problematic given that all levers of power were in the hands of the most corrupt person in the land. Mahathir had already dethroned three pervious deputy prime ministers. Would Anwar's efforts to undermine the overindulgences of Mahathir lead to his downfall?

There were serious differences between the two, and Mahathir had begun to flex his muscles.

Mahathir was a cold and maniacally shrewd politician who was not known for keeping around those who had outlived their use. Anwar's moves as education minister fed the old man's appetite for political capital, but as finance minister, now just at his heels, he had demonstrated an incorruptibility that was incompatible with the endemic corruption of the New Malaysia that Mahathir had crafted in his own image. Merryl spent endless time talking and discussing Malaysian politics. While Anwar was keen for the top job, Merryl was even more eager to see him in the prime minister's office. 'It is my main desire in life', she declared.

One day, we met Anwar in his office. We talked at length about his problems with Mahathir. He said he was moving as cautiously as possible, but the sheer extent of sleaze and crony corruption of the 'old man'—named after the Old Man of the Mountain, who led the Order of Assassins—was forcing his hand. With a rather pensive look on his face, he said: 'you are not there till you are *there*!'

The following morning, I remember rather well, I got up to see Merryl sitting at the dining table, cup of coffee in hand. She looked haggard. I thought she had experienced another one of her illustrious sleepless nights. 'Meeraal', I shouted, 'are you awake?' 'I have been thinking', she replied after a long pause. 'About the Indian Ocean World! The more you are going to think about it the more you are unlikely to write the bloody book'. 'No, no, no', she yelled. 'No'. 'I have been thinking: what could the old man do to stop Anwar from getting *there*?'

We immediately set to work on the question. We read whatever we could find by and about the old man, local and international news stories, interviews and profiles to try and work out how his mind worked. We made extensive notes on the rumour mills around Kuala Lumpur. We talked to friends and foes of Anwar to solicit their opinions. And we ploughed through works on Malaysian political history. Finally, we produced what we called 'Unthinkables'—six scenarios that the old man could use to undermine Anwar.

It was no good accusing Anwar of corruption: his integrity was unimpeachable. There was little point in accusing him of having an affair: it was not an uncommon practice among Malay politicians. It had to be something that the Malays, especially the rural brand, would find particularly reprehensible. The scenario labelled 'Unthinkable 3' anticipated that Anwar would be accused of homosexuality, perhaps involving coercion. It turned out to be farsighted.

5

After a stormy cabinet meeting, Anwar was unceremoniously dismissed by Mahathir on 2 September 1998. Masked and heavily armed men broke into his house and arrested him at gunpoint. He was savagely beaten up. One of our friends and colleagues, an advisor to Anwar, Munawar Ahmad Anees, was also arrested. Other advisors, friends and colleagues of Anwar were being rounded up. So I was following the tragedy from London. Hysterical calls to Merryl were made, begging her to come back to London. She refused.

A few days later, the phone rang in the middle of the night. 'Prof Zia?', asked the voice at the other end of the phone. I recognised it. It was Nasaruddin Jalil, Anwar's political secretary. 'Nasar' as he was known, was a short, slim man, with a perpetual grin on his face. He was always planning and making a deal. His political instincts were as sharp as his mind. 'Get Merryl out! NOW!', the voice said, and then he terminated the call. I knew I had to act immediately. But there was no point ringing Merryl.

I rang a mutual friend. 'Dr Beverage', as Merryl used to call him, taught information technology at the Mara Institute of Technology. A member of St. David's Society and a frequent visitor to Merryl's film weekends, he regularly organised lavish soirees for the expat community. Whatever the event, he took full charge of the drinks (I am told he used to make a killer Martini). Would you, I asked, kidnap Merryl and get her out of Malaysia? He admired Merryl and was aware of the dangerous nature of the situation. 'Leave it to me', he replied without hesitation. From Merryl's own accounts, I learned later that he had to 'manhandle' her as she was unwilling to leave. 'If I have to be manhandled', she said, 'then I would choose Dr Beverage for the assignment'. He stuffed the boot of his car with some of Merryl's belongings and drove her past the plain clothes security men who were watching the villa to Singapore.

Merryl stayed in Singapore for two weeks campaigning on behalf of Anwar. Then, on the advice of some of our more knowledgeable Malaysian friends, moved to Batam, an Indonesian island located twenty kilometres off Singapore's south coast. She had no funds to keep her going, but fortunately she took with her the Diners Club card I kept in Kuala Lumpur for emergency use. It came in handy as she checked into a hotel with a grand view of the Strait of Singapore. She called it 'Paradise Cove'. From her new base she wrote hundreds of letters, countless press releases and tried to get in touch with anyone and everyone she could to solicit support for Anwar's campaign. She tried also to secure her belongings back in Kuala Lumpur. She engaged a lawyer and hired a packing company. But with no result. Eventually, our kitty dried up. She had to return to London. But that was tantamount to admitting defeat—something she was not used to. Anwar was in prison. Most of his advisors and supporters were in exile. Nasaruddin Jalil had escaped to Jakarta. One of our closest friends, who was an advisor and companion of Anwar as well as a journalist and businessman, Ahmad Nazri Abdullah, had his businesses confiscated or closed; he was forced to move to London with his family. There was no hope that Merryl could return to Kuala Lumpur. Justice had evaded us. She sent a CompuServe email:

> To: The Denizens of Plumpley
> Subject: Arrival imminent of She who Must be Obeyed
> Batteries needed. There be no Giblets.

So, after twelve years in Malaysia and fifteen months on Batam, at the end of 1999, Merryl said goodbye to 'Paradise Cove' and flew to London.

I could not contain myself when I saw her. She had gained considerable weight. Her face was disfigured. Stress and anxiety had led her to endlessly grind her teeth and clench her jaws. Most of her teeth had fallen, or were loose. Her finger nails were all chewed. We hugged each other and cried. 'I look like a *hantu*' (Malay ghost), she joked. But she could not hide her pain. Her world had collapsed. She had lost everything—her treasured *objets*, her carefully curated library, her cherished video collection. She was penniless. 'Chappu', she said, 'what is to be done?'

After a few days in London, she went to Merthyr and became a recluse. She would not answer my calls and when she did she wouldn't (or couldn't) speak. I dealt with my angst in my own way by putting Anwar's story and my relationship with Kuala Lumpur on paper. The result: *The Consumption of Kuala Lumpur*, which was published in 2000. But what I could not do was to let Merryl stay in Merthyr and wallow in her sorrow. Eventually, I managed to lure her to London with a promise of a job: an appointment as the Media Officer for the Muslim Council of Britain. She stayed with my daughter, Maha. They had an extraordinary attachment to each other. Merryl first met Maha when she was only two years old; over the years, godmother and goddaughter forged themselves into a combined entity. As an infant, whenever Maha saw Merryl, she would yell 'Meeraal' and jump onto her lap. The practice had continued ever since; the fact that Maha was now in her twenties made no difference. They had their own mode of receptive speech and frequently engaged in long, convoluted conversations, accompanied with relentless giggles. Merryl was not keen on working for the Muslim Council of Britain. 'Too many *heavyyoon*'—folks with too much piety and a narrow outlook, she complained. But spending a year with Maha was tremendous therapy. I could see that her trauma was easing.

She left the Muslim Council of Britain and returned to Merthyr. For a while, she did odd jobs, such as writing the booklet *Islam UK*, which accompanied the BBC 2001 Islam season, and a short treatise *Darwin and Fundamentalism*. But she had no real income. I was also in rather reduced circumstances. Merryl thought about going on *Who Wants to Be a Millionaire?* She was convinced that she could win— all the way to a million. Her encyclopaedic knowledge of relevant and irrelevant facts notwithstanding, I was not convinced. She asked me to do some 'dry runs' with her, after which I had no option but to agree with her. We put her name forward and waited for the phone to ring. We tried week after week to get her on the show. But she was never called. Then, the 9/11 attacks happened.

I was at home watching the events unfold on television. A shell-shocked woman emerged from the debris and dust cloud swirling around the Twin Towers. She looked at a waiting television reporter, and asked a direct, distressed question: 'why do they hate us?' I immediately rang Merryl, who was also glued to her television. Even before I could say anything, she said, 'I heard her. Loud and clear'. And after a pause: 'we know how to answer the question, don't we?' Within a couple of days, I had secured a contract, with a decent advance, for *Why Do People Hate America*? The publishers wanted the manuscript within three months. I suggested we should treat the question as an inquiry. Merryl suggested we use Hollywood output to frame the book and rolled out a number of titles for me to secure: *The West Wing*, *Rules of Engagement*, *The Siege*, *Delta Force* and *Shane*. 'I always, always wanted to write about *Shane*', she said. I suggested the television series *Alias* (motto: 'sometimes the truth hurts'), which I was following. She complained: 'Chappu, stop lowering my standards with all these terrible American action films'. But I insisted, and she eventually agreed. We set to work and completed the task in the designated time. The book came out in April 2002 and was an international best seller.

Success and a modicum of financial security brought her mojo back. She wanted to write a follow up to *Why Do People Hate America*? The publishers were keen on the idea. But I was working on another project—*Desperately Seeking Paradise*—and suggested that she took a break. It came in the form of a tour of Nigeria, courtesy of the British Council.

She arrived in Kano in the middle of the controversial Amina Lawal cases, which were on the front page of every newspaper. On 22 March 2002, an Islamic Shariah court in Funtua, Nigeria, sentenced Lawal, a beautiful young woman, to death by stoning for conceiving a child out of wedlock. Merryl wasted no time in seeing the head of the sharia council of Nigeria. 'A very personable medical doctor', she said. 'As Muslims we are united in agreeing Islam means peace', she told him,

> that we are not a religion or people dedicated to lopping of hands and stoning women to death. We say Sharia defines our culture and the future for our society. But when Sharia is instituted lo and behold the first thing that happens is a woman tried for adultery. The nefarious activities of men go unchecked. Do you think a just God would approve of such an unjust deed?

He assured her that he would convey her message to the sharia council and do his utmost to ensure that the judgement of the lower court would be thrown out. And it was. By the time Merryl sat down to write our second book on America, *American Dream, Global Nightmare*, Lawal's sentence was overturned by Katsina State Sharia Court of Appeal on 25 September 2003. By now, we were working together like a finely tuned machine. We talked every morning, wrote for most the day and gave progress reports to each other in the evening. Apart from finishing *American*

Dream, Global Nightmare, we also wrote *The No-Nonsense Guide to Islam*. We were going to move on to other projects. But Merryl's mother, Maisey, slipped on ice just outside her home and broke her leg. Merryl now had the responsibility to look after her.

At about the same time, Anwar came out of prison. Our attentions reverted towards him. There was a tear-jerking reunion at Nazri's London house, near Queensway. Anwar became visiting fellow at St. Anthony's College, Oxford, and Nazri hosted many more meetings at his house. Nazri was also a regular visitor to my house, and Merryl would travel from Merthyr to see him. He is an exceptionally jovial individual, always smiling and chortling—even in times of adversity. He is half-a-hafiz: someone who has memorised half of the Qur'an, and he recites the Qur'an beautifully. Apart from his glasses and a fine insignia moustache, Nazri's facial furniture also includes a distinguished scar. It does not announce its presence effortlessly—one has to look closely to note its charisma. I asked him: how did you manage to get that scar? 'According to my mum', Nazri related,

I was caught by fire at the age of four at a wedding gathering in our village. In those days, there was no electricity in the village, and we used gasoline lamps during festivals. One of the lamps ran out of gasoline and needed refuelling. The person refuelling the lamp was ignorant. Instead of waiting for the burner to cool down, he poured the spirit and lit it with matches. The lamp blew up. I was playing close by and got caught in the ensuing fire. They took me to the hospital. I vaguely remember my head was wrapped for quite some time and I could not play with other kids.

But the scar did not dampen Nazri's indefatigable spirit. 'The scar gave me aspiration to struggle and work hard. Never looked back. *Alhamdulillah.* I was the first boy from my kampung to enter University of Malaya in 1972. I still remember my family and relatives congregating at Alor Setar Railway Station to send me off to Kuala Lumpur'. He went on to become an illustrious journalist, becoming editor of the Malay newspaper, *Bertia Harian*; his career was brought to an abrupt end with the arrest of Anwar in September 1998.

We dubbed the meetings with Nazri 'what is to be done?' gatherings, devoted as they were to discussion of political strategy, the progress of the National Justice Party (KEADILAN) which Anwar established while in prison and the overall direction of 'Reformasi', the reform movement in Malaysia. Anwar could not return to politics until his disqualification—a product of imprisonment—expired in 2008. He used the time to establish his credentials as a global statesman and gained appointments at John Hopkins and Georgetown Universities. He joined his friend Al Gore, the former US Vice President, to work on the climate emergency, promote democracy in the Middle East and shape more just and humane futures.

Meanwhile, Merryl wanted to write a third book, but I had had enough of America. 'Chappu', she said, 'it should be a trilogy'. I had signed up to work on an experimental blog for the *Guardian* and wanted to devote all my time to 'Blogging the Qur'an'. She insisted, and we agreed on a compromise. She would help with the blog: 'I will make sure you don't commit calumnious follies', she declared. I insisted that the analysis in the third book, *Will America Change*, should be based on history and politics rather than film. And I would write the blog and send it to her to check for accuracy and 'follies' before submitting to the *Guardian*. She would send drafts of the chapters, with gaps clearly marked for my additions, which would be returned for editing and polishing. She kept adding film analysis, I kept deleting them, and it went on like this for a whole year as we simultaneously worked on the two projects.

By the time *Will America Change* came out, Anwar was back in Malaysia campaigning in the 2008 General Election. However, the election was held a month before his disqualification from politics had expired to deliberately exclude him from contesting a seat. A few months later, he contested in a byelection and returned to parliament. His party, KEADILAN, had done well but did not secure a majority, and his attempts to form a majority coalition did not succeed. There were other concerns. The growing support for his party was seen as a direct threat by his detractors. They resorted to the tried and tested tactic:

fabricated accusations of 'sodomy' began to surface yet again. In July 2008, he was arrested once more; there was a long, drawn-out court case, and Anwar was finally acquitted in 2012.

Merryl followed the events in Malaysia very closely. As her mobility went the way of the Dodo, Merryl adapted to keep herself in the know. This began with nearly constantly having one news outlet or the other on in the background, an ambience of information. When the UK stations went to sleep, the US networks kept the pace until dawn. When she wasn't judging the flaws of each broadcast, she was analysing how the events would unfold. She also had a preternatural ability to connect with people and extract gossip and opinions on a variety of matters. Her network was strongest among those who remained in Malaysia, particularly the expat community, who regularly reported to her developments left out by the largely state-controlled Malaysian news outlets. But there were also concerns close to home.

Her mother was in and out of the hospital and required close, full-time attention. Then, in February 2009, Maisey died. At her funeral, Merryl described her mother as 'a lady who took the trouble to listen, to read and to reflect about her way of faith and mine'. She contributed her zest for life and enthusiasm to her job as director of the Merthyr Tydfil Institute for Blind, the volunteer organisation Soroptimists and to fellowship at Christ Church and many other local organisations. Her portrait has pride of place in the institute's office in Merthyr.

Distraught at the loss of her mother, and confined to Merthyr for a number of years, Merryl wanted to 'go somewhere completely different'. I was going to Pakistan to work on an issue of the left-wing international magazine, *New Internationalist*. She decided to accompany me.

In July 2010, Pakistan suffered 'the worst flood in living memory'. Heavy monsoon rains devastated the country. Around one-fifth of Pakistan's land was underwater. When we arrived in Karachi in March 2011, the north-west frontier state of Khyber Pakhtunkhwa, which had suffered the brunt of damage and casualties, had still not fully recovered. The first questions she raised were utterly typical: what effect did the flood have on Pakistan's historic site Mohenjo Daro, the city build around the twenty-sixth century BC and the cradle of Indus Valley civilisation, and the historic site of Taxila, the largest continually occupied urban settlement in the world? And did pervious floods lead to the end of the Indus Valley civilisation? She wanted to travel to Mohenjo Daro. But then changed her mind and decided to visit a remote village in Khyber Pakhtunkhwa: Pir Sabaq, which was under water for seventeen days. It was going to be a hazardous journey, and I was not too keen. But, as usual, she had her own way.

At Pir Sabaq she found the echoes of her own life. 'The sudden deluge sent its 6,000 inhabitants running for their lives', she wrote. 'They left behind everything they owned. From the barren mountains where they took refuge, they viewed the total devastation of the lives they had known', she wrote.

> As I walked around the village there was total absence of the normal agricultural sounds and smells of livestock. For a farming village it is multiple loss: a source of transport, power to plough and work machines, milk as well as meat—it all has to be replaced or substituted from outside for money, which is in as short supply as the beasts of the fields ... I (saw) just one, scrawny ox hitched to a cart. When Noah began again, he at least had two!

She was interested in how the women rebuilt their lives, and she lived with them for a number of days. Being stripped bare of everything is unimaginable, incomprehensible, she said. There are no more savings, no nest eggs to rely on, no family members from whom to borrow, no credit rating, few jobs to be had and everyone is in the same boat, or rather without a boat to float.

She returned from Pir Sabaq to Karachi much disturbed. The plight of the village clearly affected her. She only smiled when my relatives called her 'Begum Sahiba'—respected Begum. The smile became a grin when she was referred to as 'memsahib', an appellation reserved for white foreign women of social standing. How ironic, I thought. This was someone who had fought all her life against colonialism and imperialism. And here she was being addressed as though she was a wife of a British colonial administrator. But she did not mind. She was thinking about her own deprivations. The loss of her mother. Everything she left behind in Kuala Lumpur. And her concerns for Anwar, who was, once again, being politically dispossessed. Her own history had come back to hound her. She became very ill. We had to stay in Pakistan till she had somewhat recovered.

A few weeks after our return from Pakistan, Merryl rang. 'Chappu, don't panic!', she said. 'I am having a heart attack. The ambulance is on its way'. Before I could reply, the ambulance had arrived, and she put the phone down. I spent a couple of hours pacing my attic room. The phone rang again. 'I am on my way to operation theatre. Don't bother coming to Merthyr. I will call you when it is all over'. After a week, she was back home. She acquired a measure of cheerfulness and accepted the position as director of the newly relaunched Muslim Institute in London—a learned society of fellows. The Muslim Institute had been around since the early 1970s. But it got caught in politics, and then became snared in the trap of ideology. Merryl helped relaunch it as an institution fit for the twenty-first century. She also helped to shape the institute's quarterly *Critical Muslim*, which was started in 2012. The fellows of the institute came to adore her as she regaled them with her wit and banter year after year at the institute's annual winter gatherings. Back in her element, she started writing regularly for the *Critical Muslim*. But Malaysia was always on her mind.

In the 2013 Malaysian general election, Anwar led a coalition as the leader of the opposition. The coalition won 50.9 per cent of the popular vote, but this was not enough for him to dethrone the incumbents. There were allegations of gerrymandering; Anwar also alleged that extensive electoral fraud had taken place. There was little doubt in our mind: once again, Anwar presented a clear and present danger to the ruling elite. Within a year of the election, the incumbent government started conspiring against him. The sequel to his 'sodomy' case, Sodomy II as the legal aficionados in Malaysia had dubbed it, had not quite found its conclusion.

We met Anwar at a London hotel on a bitterly cold morning in February 2014. By now the plot against him was in full swing. There was to be a hearing at the court of appeal. The government was going to contest his acquittal on the second sodomy charge. We pleaded with him not to go back to Malaysia. 'Stay in London', Merryl said. 'We can carry on the fight from here'. But Anwar brushed our concerns aside. It was, he said, a matter of principle for him to return to Malaysia. 'Don't worry', he said with his customary grin, 'I will be alright. Their appeal will be rejected'. But under government pressure, the court of appeal suddenly decided that the earlier high court acquittal did not critically evaluate the evidence against him. The acquittal was overturned, and Anwar was back, for the third time in his life, in prison.

History was repeating itself. First time it was a farce. Now? Well, we were forced, after Hal Foster, to ask, *What Comes After Farce?* Foster was concerned about left wing cultural politics; we were anxious about Malaysian politics and Anwar's future. Merryl immediately launched into campaign mode. Meetings were held with Nazri and members of Anwar's party. Letters were written. Western politicians and journalists were contacted. Articles were published. But our efforts were futile.

We were broken like a shattered pot. Merryl found it difficult to write. She was constantly ill. The skin on her left leg became blistered. Then tumid. After a few months, the right leg also got infected. Both her legs were now swollen and painful. She was diagnosed with cellulitis and given antibiotics and cream to rub on her legs. It did not work. More antibiotics followed to no avail. She found it difficult to walk. She could not continue her work as the director of the Muslim Institute. She was asked to write an introductory text on anthropology. Something that she would have taken in her stride was now a daunting task. She struggled for months.

A perpetual air of melancholy shrouded her.

Scars can be worn as a badge of pride, as Nazri showed. Broken pots can be restored to become more beautiful and stronger than ever.

6

Nazri rang. I was in Istanbul, in a car, on my way to a workshop in a rural part of Turkey. 'We are on our way to win the election', he announced. It was May 2018. A few days later, Pakatan Harapan, the coalition that Anwar formed as a leader in absentia, became the new government. Within a week, Anwar was granted a royal pardon and released from prison. There was a problem. The new prime minister was none other than Anwar's old adversary, Mahathir Mohamad. The leaders of Pakatan Harapan had decided that in the absence of Anwar, the 'old man' would be interim prime minister. His wife, Wan Azizah Wan Ismail, who had stood by Anwar and courageously faced all the tribulations visited on her, her husband and her party by the 'old man', as well as those who succeeded him, would be deputy prime minister.

Anwar asked Merryl to return to Kuala Lumpur. A 'spacious and luxurious' room in his office building was prepared for her. She arrived to find herself in a sparsely furnished large room, with an attached bathroom. 'More like spartan than luxurious', she said. By now, cellulitis had taken a permanent hold on her legs. But she was back in her element, holding court in her room, drafting speeches, providing bountiful advice and engaging in long, convoluting arguments—always with a cigarette in hand and flask of coffee by her side. The television in her room would be permanently on as she would be half-listening to BBC World or CNN. Anwar would drop in for an involved conversation (sometimes of a political nature, sometimes of literary bent) and would be criticised frankly but lovingly as well as handed a list of references to consult. Sometimes she would sneak out to share a cigarette and gossip with Nazri.

Even though she had difficulty walking, she loved going out for 'food and beverage'. She had developed an affectionate connection with our young colleague, Scott Jordan. Long lectures on the history of Malaya, Wales, the evils of the British Empire, the subtle art of *objet* curation and, of course, the Indian Ocean World were visited on the poor chap. Scott, who took her out on regular shopping expeditions, had picked up our lingo and engaged with Merryl in our trademark repartee. That, no doubt, brought them even closer. The best place for 'food and beverage' was undoubtedly Nazri's (late and lamented) restaurant, Symphony. We would gather there frequently for lavish dinners, accompanied by generous amounts of Shariah-compliant wine, heated arguments, the latest political gossip and scintillating conversations till closing time. For a while, it looked like the happy times of the 1980s and 1990s had returned.

Merryl saw her work as repairing what was done to Anwar and Malaysia, a process of restoration that transforms loss to recovery, tragedy to triumph. A bit like *kintsugi*, the Japanese technique of repairing broken pots. The pots are repaired with lacquer and gold. While the cracks are all too visible, the pots are restored to their original function, but now, with the added beauty of gold, they become works of art. They tell stories. There was much to do to take Anwar's story forward; just as she obsessed over making a trilogy out of the America books, she took to seeing Anwar's trilogy not as one of sodomy show trials but as the proper rise, fall and transcendence of the hero's journey—more attuned to the old films they bonded over. She devoted all her energies to the required work.

We worked on delineating Anwar's vision for Malaysia. We turned his vision into a policy framework based on sustainability, care and compassion, mutual respect, innovation and the Malay notion of prosperity that seeks to balance material growth with spiritual fulfilment. We developed plans and future scenarios. But there was a nagging doubt. Will Mahathir hand over power to Anwar? Anwar had publicly forgiven Mahathir and was convinced that he had changed. We were not persuaded. Mahathir was dillydallying. 'Do scorpions act against their nature?', Merryl asked pointedly. As the famous Sufi parable of a frog and a scorpion illustrates—they don't.

During Christmas of 2019, Merryl went to South Africa to attend a wedding and spend time with her niece. On the return Qatar Airways flight to Kuala Lumpur she fell seriously ill, was removed from the plane at Doha and taken to hospital. She woke up in an intensive care unit.

Several days had passed, and she was now in a different year than the one she was last conscious in. For a couple of days, we had no idea where she was. Frantic phone calls were made before she was traced. A week later she was cleared to depart from Doha. When she eventually got back to Kuala Lumpur, she was a different woman. Her legs were badly swollen because of lymph fluid buildup. Bandages on her legs had to be changed on a daily basis. A nurse, Grace, was appointed to perform the task. Drying agents were applied to tame the swelling, followed by lotions to sooth the dead skin and reduce the swelling. Wan Azizah, the one force on this earth Merryl would instantly give in to (at mere mention of Wan Azizah's impending arrival, she would put out the cigarette she was in the middle of and hide any remaining stragglers), had enlisted friends and professionals to completely rewrite her diet. She was put on a cocktail of medicine—Western and non-western! It was an indication that her body was battered beyond endurance.

The relationship between Anwar and Mahathir was also in intensive care. Towards the end of 2019, we developed a set of political scenarios. The worst scenario, entitled 'Full Metal Jacket', suggested that Mahathir would—once again—declare war on Anwar and use all in his means to prevent him from ascending to power. When the scenario was presented to Anwar, he refused to think about or engage with it. He was still convinced that Mahathir would keep his word and move out of the prime minister's office so he could move in.

Yet again, history was moving in cycles. And no one was more concerned than Merryl. But it wasn't just Malaysian politics that was repeating the mistakes of the past; the world itself was also treading the same course. The most problematic thing we inherit from the past, Merryl said, is how we think about our problems. 'We cannot resolve our problems with more of the same, simply using the same old ideas that helped produce our present problems. We have to understand how we came to think about our economy, politics, the world system, nature and the environment, as we do. We have to trace the roots of our way of thinking to realise there are other possibilities, different ways to understand the problems, and think about their solution'. We need to learn to ask new questions, she emphasised.

The question regarding Mahathir was settled. He declared full scale assault on Anwar, just as our scenario suggested. The carefully restored pot began to fall apart. In a series of political manoeuvres, in which Mahathir and Anwar's former allies played a sinister role, Pakatan Harapan lost power. Anwar was the leader of the opposition, *de novo*. On top of that, the Covid-19 pandemic had arrived. The new back-door government took advantage, declared a state of emergency and locked down the entire country—ensuring Anwar was as far as possible from power. The psychological impact on Merryl is difficult to judge. I was stuck in London experiencing its own Covid confusion and paranoia, including wine and cheese parties at 10 Downing Street. Merryl was trapped in Kuala Lumpur. The ghosts of 1998 had re-emerged with vengeance. Merryl was clearly shattered. She confined herself to her room. This state of affairs lasted nearly two years. But even after pandemic precautions were eased, she refused all of Scott's and other friends' invitations to go out for dinner or to socialise with others.

Her legs were now weeping profusely. She had to be taken to hospital. The solution was standard, a course of antibiotics. But Merryl was beyond the usual antibiotics, she required the 'nuclear bomb' of antibiotics, full course. Each run truly took it out of her. While being treated for her legs, she had a setback and was moved to an intensive care unit. Her condition deteriorated rapidly. Doctors told us to prepare for the worst. It appeared that the team of specialists now seeing to her were running out of options. There was fear that the bugs we were dealing with were resistant to the available antibiotics. Also, the toll on her body was beginning to push an already weakened heart. They were engaged in a balancing act of applying enough antibiotics to take on the multiple bacterial infections in her system while also using blood pressure regulators at the right dosage to keep her heart functional. We waited and prayed.

For several days, the less news was for the better. In prior hospitalisations she would jest about how the placard could be changed outside her spacious and luxurious room like the one changed at the gates of Buckingham Palace informing the public of the condition of the royal family. Now we would get daily updates in the form of WhatsApp messages from nurse Grace and her attending physicians. Due to the complications of the Covid-19 pandemic, visitation was highly limited. Scott managed to see her and review her condition. He found her between spouts of consciousness, but this did not deter his mission to report the multipage list of the headlines that he knew she'd be without in her ICU room. He also managed to play Mike Oldfield's Tubular Bells for her on my request. My constant playing of the song in our various residences drove Merryl to develop disdain for the tune. The logic was that on hearing only a few notes of the song, she would have to return to consciousness, if only to give the coldest death stare to the perpetrator of the artistic crime. Slowly her moments of consciousness improved to interactions and vocal communication. She was recovering. We had a video chat. She looked warped. 'Hello!', she said. 'I am here. I am still with you. You are not going to get rid of me yet'. Doctors instructed her to stop smoking. 'Let me think about it', she replied.

A few days later, doctors announced that she was well on her way to recovery. Her 'spacious and luxurious' room was now restructured, turned into a two-bedroom flat and furnished according to her taste, with extra facilities to help her mobility. Anwar even managed to stop by and see her. She was conscious and awake when he arrived, in the middle of one of the twice-a-day sessions with the doctors. Anwar was amazed. He had only seen pictures that indicated the worst during this stay, and the last thing he expected was to see Merryl in her element, witty as ever, expecting updates on the political situation while also critiquing the comfort of the numerous hospital beds she had been in, none of them qualifying as comfortable. Anwar was happy to see her joking and smiling, but when she gave him time to speak, he had important words for her. 'Merryl, things are going to have to change. We need you healthy. Your diet and lifestyle. No more smoking!' Anwar waited for the expected retort. The 'No, no, no, no' followed by an 'Excuzzee!' But instead, she smiled, closed her eyes, and put her hand on her heart. 'Yes Mr. Prime Minister. Alhamdulillah!' The room was colonised by silence as the army of medical professionals taking readings and changing tubes were frozen. Merryl would slip back to sleep after the utterance. Anwar was dumbfounded. These would be the last words she would say to him.

On 1 February 2021, she returned to her base, with Nurse Grace in attendance. She had a video chat with Maha and I. She was lying in bed, appeared calm, albeit a little confused. 'Get some rest', we said. 'Talk to you tomorrow, be be!', she replied. Immediately afterwards, she asked Grace to help her move over to the other side of the bed. She had another heart attack and took her final breath as she was being moved.

Pandemic restrictions still kept the world largely in an inert state. Her body had to be tested for Covid. Thankfully she was negative, and a few individuals were allowed to attend her funeral. But many watched on Zoom as Scott broadcast the proceeding via his mobile. I watched from London with Saliha and Maha. We cried as we huddled together. She was buried in a beautiful hillside. Not too far from the Malaysian Parliament, where Malaysian democracy remained in the hands of corrupt and greedy politicians.

She shined wherever she went. She enriched my life and every life she touched. She leaves us faded by her terrestrial absence. But she will be a constant intellectual and spiritual presence on the rest of my days. Her intellectual legacy will, to use her favourite word, endure.

In moments of solitude, I imagine she is having a pleasant but protracted argument with God.

I murmur: '*Ye, ye, Meraal. Said Qi?*' She replies: '*Ye, ye, Chappu! Systi Ok*'. Why should a mere thing like death separate us?

Saliha

1

'*Meri jaan*'.

That's what I called her. When she was anxious or concerned about something: *meri jaan*, my life, my love. I would put my arms around her. She was not a natural hugger. Her first reaction would be to hold back. But once I clasped and held her firmly, she would calm down; her worries would melt away. We would become one. A single life.

Usually, she was Begum. It was, as I was eventually to discover, part of her name. Her birth certificate has her name as 'Saliha Begum'. It is an honorific given to Muslim women of high social or cultural standing in South Asia. Sometimes it is just added to the first name without a solid reason. In Saliha's family there are many Begums. Her mother and aunts are Begums. But by the time she got married and had Sardar added to her name, Begum had been dropped. Her first passport, issued in Multan, Pakistan, on 27 December 1977, has Saliha Basit (her father's name) written underneath her photograph in blue ink, with Sardar added in black, as though an afterthought. But I called her Begum: she was my Begum, my queen, my wife, my beloved, who elevated my position, gave honour and dignity to my life.

My nephews and nieces, and some younger members of our extended family, called her 'Dulhan'—Bride. When we were getting married, my nephew, Atif, who was two years old, asked: who is the woman sitting on the podium, wrapped in red garments. She is the Dulhan, he was told. He, and other children present at the wedding, started to call her Dulhan. The appellation stuck.

But she was appropriately named and was always Saliha—the virtuous one. It is a Qur'anic term that also means righteous, pious and just. In its different forms, the word occurs a hundred times in ninety-eight verses of the Qur'an. Saliha personified righteousness. She was, according to the Qur'an, one who 'does righteous deeds and has faith' (16:97). For her, wealth and consumerism were nothing more than 'allurements of the life of this world'. She was interested in 'the things that endure' (18:46).

'Things that endure' were the virtues that were deeply engrained in her. She embodied what in Muslim history and circles is called *akhlaq*, 'character traits' that define a virtuous person. These virtues are spelled out in the Qur'an: humility, sincerity, patience, modesty, prudence, forgiveness, courage, love and justice. She did not acquire these virtues. They were infused within her by the grace of God and enhanced by her upbringing, by the traditional setting of her family background and by her own conscientious personality. She provided a counterbalance to my obvious shortcomings. I tend to be a little—some will say quite a lot—arrogant. But Saliha was totally selfless: humility positively shone in her. My patience is rather limited. In contrast, she seemed to have patience in abundance. Her humility combined with her modesty. But modesty for her was not about *hijab* or how you dress (hardly any women in her family wore the hijab). The outward manifestation of modesty was limited to her *doputtas*, which she wore like a shawl, covering her head and shoulders. Being a traditional woman, she did not really like to hug. There was always an initial reluctance even to hug her husband. 'You can just as well love me from some distance', she would say. Modesty was about how you lived, and she lived frugally, hated any kind of waste, shunned extravagance and never, never overindulged herself. Moderation defined her lifestyle. I can be harsh, particularly when dealing with annoying folks. She was as gentle as a dove and never had a bad word for anyone.

She was not an intellectual. But she symbolised the rare and unfashionable virtue of prudence, the cerebral virtue that connected and gave meaning to all her other virtues. For Saliha, it was not good enough to know what was the right thing to do. She *felt* what was the right thing to do, what was the right way to do it and when she should do it. She had an inner moral compass that not only enabled her to reflect, judge and act but to do all this within the framework of traditional Islamic ethics and morality. I tend to emphasise reasoning at the expense of feeling and, as such, am an abridged individual. Saliha was a holistic, integrated person who could think and feel what was the right thing to do and did it without reserves. She had a living awareness of reality beyond her material existence.

Every now and then, she got angry. She was always pining for children. She was unhappy that I wasn't always there when she needed me. But most of all she was livid about the discrimination she saw around her, the ever-present injustices of the world. She would get frustrated when she could not articulate her feelings. In frustration, she would exclaim: 'is there no limit to the greed of some people?' 'Why can't the refugees be treated like human beings?' 'When will the suffering of the Palestinians end?' The questions were often thrown in my direction, and she expected a satisfactory answer. 'But Begum', I would plead, 'it's not my fault that the refugees are being treated so badly'. 'I am not responsible for the war in Ukraine!' 'I am not responsible for the actions of the Israelis'. Of course, the replies were never satisfactory. Her standard retort would be: '*loog insan naheen han*'—people are not human. '*Ham main insan bana hay*'—we have to become human. Her anger was often directed towards me. But I knew that her inner disposition was always oriented to a greater good. She saw justice as our obligation to all others. Everyone had value independent of our own interests. They had to be treated with equality, compassion and love, and embraced as though they were an integral part of us. They were us.

Despite her anger at the injustices she saw all around her, those who were privileged enough to meet Saliha instantly noticed the calm, the grace and the inner and outer beauty that emanated from her.

2

I first met Saliha, my mother once told me, when I was seven.

In those days, most of my extended family lived in Bahawalnagar, a town just east of the Sutlej River, the longest of the five rivers that flow through the crossroads of Punjab—the land of the five waters. Saliha's parents lived with their parents, and other members of the large family, in a two-bedroom house in the centre of the town, towards the end of the Railway Bazaar, the main street. The family had arrived in Bahawalnagar after partition and the traumas of the perilous migration—during which members of the family faced riots, attacks, were lost, presumed dead, and found—were fresh and deep.

Upon his arrival in Pakistan, Saliha's father, Abdul Basit Khan, immediately enrolled in the Air Force. He served for twelve years and then resigned because of 'beard issues'. He joined the local police department but could not tolerate the corruption he saw all around him and left after a couple of years. Finally, he became secretary of the union council to the district of Bahawalnagar. Her mother, Zubaida Begum, became the principal of a nearby primary school, where she remained until her retirement. Basit and Zubaida married in their late teens, as traditional families tended to do, and in some cases still do.

They lived in the house of Abdul Raziq Khan—known to all as *nana*, grandfather, although sometimes I called him Dada—who was a noted pre-partition judge in Punjab. His elder brother, Abdul Khaliq Khan, served as a minister to the nawab of Hyderabad, Deccan. And, his maternal uncle, Maloof Khan, was an internationally famous hunter. But all that was in 'India'; the illustrious family history became irrelevant in Pakistan. Abdul Raziq Khan, a trained *hakim*, opened his surgery in Railway Bazaar and started practicing. Eventually he became a celebrated 'Hakim Sahib' of Bahawalnagar. Saliha was born in Hakim Sahib's house on 29 January 1958. She was the eldest child and only daughter of Abdul Basit Khan and Zubaida Begum, who had four sons after her: Abdul Majid Khan, Abdul Wajid Khan, Abdul Qadar Khan and Abdul Mumin Khan.

I lived with my parents in Depalpur, an ancient town about eighty miles north of Bahawalnagar. We shared our modest dwelling with my mother's youngest brother, Shahid. When the news of Saliha's birth reached Depalpur, the whole family, which by now also included my sister, Huma, then three years old, got on a bus to see the newly born. It was perhaps one of the most dangerous journeys of my life. It took about five hours on a narrow, single lane, bumpy road, where horrendous accidents were not unknown. The bus driver, under the influence of whatever he incessantly chewed (a mildly intoxicating tobacco, or hashish, I later learned), drove at great speed with little care. When we entered the bus, he pointed to a warning calligraphed on the inside: 'Remember God! And pray. Before they pray on your grave'. I sat, with my young uncle Shahid and the other children at the front of the bus, shouting at the bus driver to avoid approaching potholes and on-coming traffic. The passengers exhaled a loud sigh of relief on reaching the destination and, indeed, prayed in unison, thanking God for their safe arrival.

As soon as we entered Hakim Sahib's house, the entire visiting family rushed to kiss and embrace the baby—almost suffocating her in the process. She was passed like a valued parcel from person to person. As one of the youngest, I was last in the queue. She was carefully handed to me, with my mother watching over me to ensure that I did not, unconsciously or enthusiastically, mishandle or drop her.

Over the next year, we travelled a few times to Bahawalnagar. I used to play with Saliha and carry her on my shoulders, my mother says. Then, my parents moved to Sahiwal (known in those days as Montgomery). Soon afterwards, we migrated to Hackney, London. And I did not see Saliha for almost twenty years.

In Bahawalnagar, the extended family tried to establish its roots. But making a new life in a new place was not easy and sent family members hiving off in all directions scrambling to find jobs and opportunity. Some moved to Lahore, some to Karachi. Saliha's parents stayed in Bahawalnagar, where she went to school. Later, she moved to Lahore to attend the Government Model College for Girls, Model Town. The family was rather poor and could not afford to pay her fees. So, on 12 October 1974, she wrote a letter to the Principal of the College:

> Madam—I am the student of 11 years in the Government Model College for Girls under your kind control. The income of my father is very small, and he has to support a large family. The prices of every commodity these days is abnormally high, and it is very difficult for him to make both ends meet. I may add for your kind attention that I belong to a teacher's family and many members of the family are attached with the education department.
>
> I, therefore, request you kindly to grant me fee concession.
>
> I shall be highly thankful to your kindness.
> Yours obediently,
> Saliha Basit

I don't know whether the 'fee concession' was granted. But I do know that the family was facing hardship and, with the spread of family members all over Pakistan, and with my own family's migration to London, there was another concern. The bonds of family that were the matrix of their lives seemed to be weakening. To some extent, my mother Hamida and Saliha's mother Zubaida had anticipated this. The sisters were uprooted from all the normality they had known. They had suffered the trauma of partition, which had by now become an integral part of their selves. Now they faced the dispersion of loved family members. So the sisters hatched a plan, before partition and just after they married, to reverse the global forces that were shattering their tradition—not so much ritual and practices to which both were devoted, but the essence that shaped their identity, the core values and ideas that told them who they really were and how they could relate to the changing world around them. They agreed that their first-born children, if they were a boy and a girl, would marry each other. This way, they could preserve the family bonds, even when different members of the family were located in different parts of the world, and pass on to their offspring the solidity and support of the certainties the sisters had once known.

The sisters were resilient and tenacious. They had a particular notion of family: an institution to share and ease burdens, to support and encourage and to provide the safety net that does not permit people to fall through the cracks. For them, a family was your counsellor, helper, diversion, a source of company and society that does not judge and reject however much it may comment, nag, harangue and in infinite variety surround you with unending streams of opinion for your own good, whether it's the good you agree with or not. And they were determined to implement their plan and promise. But neither ever mentioned their cherished scheme to the offspring concerned.

Time came when the arrangement so long planned had to be put in place. Saliha graduated from the Government Model College for Girls with a degree in psychology. I grew up to manhood to become that new creation, a British Asian. I was taken on a purposeful visit to Pakistan in 1976 and presented with the proposal. But I was told she had said 'yes'. I thought: traditional families can be quite manipulating. It was quite possible that she murmured 'no' but her no was interpreted as perhaps, maybe, and then yes. If she had remained silent when the question was asked, that too would be interpreted as yes. So, there was no option for a no.

And in any case, I was not keen to marry a cousin. We were worlds apart. She did not know me. I hardly knew her. So I did not see Saliha and said 'no'. I later learned that in fact she had said yes. But after hearing that I said no, she changed her mind and said no. But 'no' was conspicuously absent from the vocabulary of the two sisters.

I had in fact fallen in love during my visit to Pakistan. But in a different way to a different person. I discovered Munni Begum, the peerless diva of Pakistani music. I was mesmerised by her on my first encounter. I saw her as the aunty next door who would pop in at just the right time to sing the exact *ghazal* that expressed my thoughts or feelings.

Meanwhile, my mother and the other aunty in my life attempted to build a consensus. There was a lot of to-and-fro during the next year. The two sisters were well versed in the art form of nudging their children in the direction they desired. The art involved subtle manoeuvring, reiterating tragic and triumphant segments of family history and constant reminders (that have stayed with me ever since) of the important virtue of looking after the less fortunate members of the extended family. I was told that marriage in our tradition is a social act because it is not personal and individual, it never involves just two people each alone with their own angst and dreams. Marriage is much too important to be left to the precarious dreams and delusions of a would-be bride and groom. However, because a marriage involves the extended family, this does not mean it is not personal. Stop thinking in discrete boxes, my mother said, separating and partitioning, as you are missing the point. Extended families and their collective actions do not eradicate the individuality of each member. On the contrary, they place an emphasis on the idiosyncrasies, the personhood, of each member. An extended family is, par excellence, the safe and secure environment in which to stake your ground for being exactly who you are and to be accepted as such. One is an abstract unit of a social abstraction. Instant love is an illusion; love grows as a couple bond, grow as a unit, to make a life together. No soul, let alone a twenty-six-year-old, I thought, can survive such an onslaught.

Inevitably, I returned to Pakistan in 1977. My arrival in Karachi was already being seen as an affirmative action. The entire extended family settled in Karachi accompanied me to Bahawalnagar. *Charpais*—traditional woven beds—were laid out outside Hakim Sahib's house for the visiting men to sleep on. I spent a sleepless night on a *charpai* fighting off a battalion of mosquitoes.

The following morning, I got up to go to the toilet. It was a small closet in a corner of the veranda. I entered, accompanied by a *lota*—a brass round-shaped vessel that resembles a tea pot—and sat awkwardly on two small pillars. The end product dropped on a container underneath. Not accustomed to squatting, it was not an easy manoeuvre to perform. As I was trying to unsuccessfully balance myself, a hand emerged from underneath the pillars and pulled the container away. I was shocked. Froze. Cleaned myself quickly, using the lota water, as best as I could. And came out onto the veranda to rapturous laughter.

I had entered the closet while it was being cleaned. Apparently, the cleaner had made the usual announcement at the beginning of the process, but I was unaware. Amongst the gathering in the veranda was Saliha, carrying a *balti* of water. There was a sublime smile on her face. There was also a grace and beauty that astonished me. I was mesmerised.

'Oay', I shouted to attract her attention. 'Do you think I would make a reasonable husband?' 'Probably', she shouted back, 'but not for me'. Then she threw the *balti* of water over me!

I was always married to Saliha. Even before I was married. Even before I was born.

3

Hakim Sahib was well known, and people were keen to attend the wedding of his granddaughter. So, invited or not, virtually half of the then population of Bahawalnagar was there. A 'Mehndi' ceremony was held. The women of the household decorated the bride with henna. It was all done with consummate skill: all varieties of pattern and flora and fauna were created on the hands and feet of the bride. The wedding itself was a modest affair. I had to wear a *shalwar kurta* suit, an Afghan *topi* on my head, and garlands of tinsel and flowers around my neck. She wore the traditional red wedding dress, adorned with jewellery. Not that I saw her. While I was outside in a tent, she was in a room inside the house. A young local mullah arrived with a huge register. He asked me three times whether I accepted Saliha Basit as my wife. I replied '*jee haan*' (yes sir) every time. Then, he went inside the house and asked Saliha if she accepted Ziauddin Sardar as her husband. She took her time to reply, then whispered '*jee haan*'. The Mullah was not sure or did not hear. 'Can't hear you', he said. She shouted: 'JEE HAAN! JEE HAAN! JEE HAAN'. Her voice reverberated so even those outside in the tent could hear it.

The Mullah filled the marriage certificate:

Nikah Nama
Form No 2.
Muslim Family Law Ordinance 1961, Bahawalnagar.
Groom's age: 27.
Bride's age: 20.
Dowry: 20,000 rupees (currency of the time).
Date: 29 Dhu'l-Hijjah 1397; 11 December 1977.
Fees paid for registration: 20 rupees.
Name of the representative of the bride (Hakim Sahib and someone else).
Names of the eight witnesses (scribble in a way that is difficult to read).

When it came to the witnesses, numerous people rushed in to sign. It was obvious that some of them were complete strangers. So, there was a commotion when the family members, neighbours and acquaintances had to be sorted from other eager witnesses. When the document was signed, the mullah tore the form from the register and handed it to Hakim Sahib. But he did a poor job; the first column of the form was left attached to the register.

The registration was followed by a sumptuous feast. A number of family members came forward to read wedding poems (*Saraas*) written for the occasion, with the names and virtues of the bride and groom sprinkled generously. At around three o'clock in the morning, I was allowed into the bridal chamber, after paying—bribing?—the women who were guarding the bride.

This is how I described what happened next in *Balti Britain*.

Once inside the room, I could not move. I stood there behind the door looking at Saliha…. Slowly, the noise and the buzz around the house subsided. Someone had put a *ghazal* on a tape recorder; clearly, I could hear Munni Begum, singing:

> *I am drinking with my eyes,*
> *Let not this atmosphere change.*
> *Do not lower your gaze*
> *For this night may fade away.*

I managed to walk a few steps and sat beside her.

> *There's still some night left*
> *Do not remove your veil.*
> *Your faltering and falling drunk*
> *May regain his balance.*

She removed her *duppata*, placed her arms around my waist and embraced me.

> *Owner of my life*
> *Put your hands on my heart*

I fear that the joy of your arrival
would stop my heart from beating.

She leaned forward, grabbed a book that was lying under the cushion and handed it to me. I read the title: *Intermediate Biology.*

Many, many years later I discovered that Saliha kept a diary. The entry for the wedding day, in Urdu, reads:

11 December 1977: On 11 December 1977 we got married and my life took a new turn. This was the most beautiful day of my life because I acquired the person I desired. In every way, Zia is ideal for me. Even though we have not seen each other for 19 years. But Zia is not a stranger to me in any way. He understands everything I say and do. Perhaps, he too desires me as much as I desire him. There is not enough time for me to write down his qualities. But I like everything he says. He has a very warm and shining personality, but he spends lot of time thinking of naughty things to do. He loves children; he is frequently seen carrying a child. He is passionate about helping the poor, the labourers and the sick. He seeks to help them as much as he can.

Wedding over, we went to Karachi. After making arrangements for her UK visa, I had to return to London. I was enormously miserable about leaving her behind. I did not know how long it would take her to get her visa and join me in London. She was even sadder. On 29 January 1978, her birthday, she wrote in her diary:

Zia, who is dearer to me than my life, left for London on the six o'clock flight in the morning. I longed for him all day; I wanted to hear his voice. To hear him call: 'Begum, Begum!' I wanted to smell his particular odour...

And again, on 4 February 1978: 'I am waiting for his letter. He must have written to me as soon as he got back'.

Saliha was granted 'leave to stay' and join her husband. But by the time she arrived in London, I had left for Jeddah where I was then working.

11 June 1978: Today, my life took a new turn. I left Pakistan and all my relatives and arrived in London. There were people at the airport to collect me. But not the one for whom I left everyone and everything behind. I missed him terribly today.

The following day, 12 June 1978: 'This is my second day in London. Only I know how I managed to pass the night without Zia. I am so close, yet so far. When will this separation end?'

The next day, 13 June 1978: 'I have all I need here. Everyone loves me. But despite it all, I want to sit quietly, and not speak to anyone. I just don't want anyone or anything in my thoughts but Zia'.

She stayed with my parents in our council house in Amberly Estate. I wrote to her regularly, encouraging her to improve her English and perhaps learn to cook. She came to London with virtually nothing. But she did bring four books: *Lazeez Khanna* (Delicious Food) by Rabia Saeed in Urdu, *Quranic Advice*, an Arabic text with translation by Marmaduke Pickthall and Urdu translation by Maulana Fateh Mohammed Jalendhari and a copy of Sura Yaseen without translation which always remained by her bedside along with a small pocket-sized booklet of *duas* (prayers).

Lazeez Khanna had a couple of well-thumbed pages. My mother must have told her about my fondness for *karelas*. That is why, I figure, when picked, *Lazeez Khanna* would automatically open on page 240, with a recipe for bitter gourd with meat:

Karela Ghost

Ingredients: Meat half *ser*. Ghee one-and-half *chhataank*. Karelas one *pao*. Cloves one *tola*. Cardamom one *tola*. Onion one *chhataank*. Ginger eight *tola*. Dry coriander one *tola*. Red pepper 1.5 *tola*. Turmeric 2.5 *maasha*.

Synthesis: Fry meat in *ghee* till it turns red. Then add onion and stir. After a little while, add water, salt, coriander and ginger, keep stirring, and cook till the meat is nice and tender. Add water if necessary. Peel the karallas, sprinkle with salt and turmeric, and put them aside in a warm place. After a while, rub them with your hands to get their bitterness out. Then rub them with yogurt and leave them aside for two to three hours. After this time, wash them with water, fry them in ghee, and mix with the meat. When they are well done, pour the garam masala. Finally, take them out of the *choola* (fireplace) and enjoy!

Lazeez Khanna uses traditional ancient South Asian units of measure which made little sense to me. The measures begin with rice: 8 grains of rice equal 1 *ratti*; 8 *ratti* equal 1 *masha*, 12 *masha* equal 1 *tola*, 5 *tola* equal one *chatank* and finally, 16 *chatank* equal one *saer* (kilogramme). They made complete sense to Saliha: it was all done by hand, a pinch here, two or three pinches there and then a handful! It all came out perfectly every time. And it was all instinct. There was an intimate connection between the hands that cooked and the hands that ate. Observing her cook made me think that our culture is not a random collection of arbitrary habits. It emerges from naturally directed instincts and is an amalgam of expressions of our instincts. Hence, the common themes across cultures, the virtues that bind us all—family, ritual, love, friendship, loyalty. For Saliha, instinct was a penchant for learning. And she learned a lot from the books she brought with her.

Apart from *karela ghost*, Saliha learned to cook *biryani* and *palou*. But her ancient shammi kebabs became legendary. The recipe is too long and complicated (and, in any case, presents a translation challenge that I cannot possibly meet). But *Lazeez Khanna* explains that just because they are called 'ancient' does not mean they are not contemporary. And *shammi* does not suggest Sham, meaning Syria. They are not Syrian in origin. 'It is just that the method used to make them was developed in the royal household of Arab, Iranian, and Indian Muslim kings; and to this day, it is the best method to make them'. Needless to say, they require much preparation.

When it came to *Quranic Advice*, she never got past the first page. Advice from part 1, chapter 1:

> And do good, surely Allah loves those who do good.
> Surely Allah loves those who turn to Him in repentance
>   and loves those who keep clean.
> Allah loves the steadfast.
> Allah loves the equitable.
> Surely Allah loves those who put their trust in Him.

But she took all the advice to heart.

4

We got married—again.

Saliha was without me for about three months. I managed to escape Jeddah and return to London in early August 1978. My father had already made an appointment for us. So we went to Westminster Town Hall for a 'civil marriage'—'Pursuant of the Marriage Act 1949'! It was not much of an affair; only my parents, brother and sister were in attendance. But it was the first time I actually looked at Saliha's Pakistani passport, which we had to present to the registrar, closely. It stated:

Colour of eyes: black
Colour of hair: black
Visible distinguishing mark: mole right side of chin.

I looked, again and again, for the said mole. It wasn't there. Anywhere.

A couple of months later, I went back to my job at the Hajj Research Centre, King Abdul Aziz University, in Jeddah. Saliha came with me. We shared a flat with my life-long friend Zafar Malik, who also worked at the Hajj Research Centre, and his wife, Sameena. The two women became the best of friends. Jeddah life was austere; there wasn't much to do, and nowhere in particular to go after work. The four us were transformed into conjoined twins, sharing our lives, frustrations and joys together. The Maliks' first child, Saad, was a source of diversion, and we took turns to look after and play with him. For us, Saad was like our own son. Occasionally, out of sheer boredom, we watched Egyptian films and soap operas on a grainy black and white television, went on evening walks on the promenade and had dinner with our colleagues at weekends, which were on Thursdays and Fridays.

While life was just about bearable for us, for the women it was intolerable. They couldn't go out on their own and were cooped up all day in our small two-bedroom flat. Worse: they had to be wrapped up in black *abayas*, faces and hair covered, looking like ghostly figures from an Edgar

Allan Poe story. Saliha longed for the freedom she enjoyed in Pakistan. 'Why do we have to wear black shrouds', she asked. 'Why can't we be simply modestly dressed?' This is Saudi Arabia, the birth place of Islam, I told her. They want women to suffer as much as possible. This is why the *abayas* are black because black is the worst colour to wear in scorching sun and flaming heat. The best colour to wear is white. That is why Saudi men *always* wear white *thawbs*.

The situation become more complicated when Saliha became pregnant. I did not want my child to be born in Saudi Arabia. So I had to take her back to London. That meant negotiating two exit visas—*khurooj*, as they are called. Not a simple task in the 1970s! Saudi Arabia does offer something unique: the opportunity to perform the Hajj. I wanted Saliha to become a Hajjan, someone who has performed the Hajj. Fortunately, the 1978 Hajj was in November and we were able to perform the Hajj together. I like to think that my eldest daughter, Maha, is also a Hajjan as Saliha was carrying her during our pilgrimage.

Perhaps 'together' is not the right word. I performed the Hajj as a research exercise: Zafar and I walked from Jeddah to Mecca, along with a rowdy donkey, tracing the old caravan route—as described in *Mecca: The Sacred City*. Saliha and Sameena went with my Hajj Research Centre colleagues. It was, as the Hajj is meant to be, a devotional activity, requiring much effort and a great deal of prayer and supplications. A genuinely humbling affair. But for us it was also a very joyous occasion, with a great deal of laughter.

Saliha returned to London soon after Hajj. We were separated again. I wanted my first child to be female, and somehow I managed to convince myself that I was going to have a daughter. I sent postcards from Jeddah with one-line messages: 'Beautiful Saliha—write to me every week. I am restless without you', or 'to the two young girls in my life'. Always signed: 'only yours'. She replied with letters in Urdu, describing her pain at being separated yet again.

The separation was just as agonising for me in Jeddah, where I was experiencing every type of bureaucratic nightmare imaginable to a mortal, making sure I had an exit visa to return to London in time for the birth. In anticipation of leaving Saudi Arabia—'desert purgatory' as I used to call it—I also started freelancing for the science journal *Nature*. Most of my free hours however were spent on reading and writing, which was not only a good use of my time but also served to ease my frustrations at Jeddah life and the agony of enforced segregation. Islamic classics were my chosen reading. I read Rumi's *Masnavi* a number of times, but seldom understood what he was getting at. It was only after I had truly experienced the angst of separation that I understood that:

> A true lover is proved such by his pain of heart
> No sickness is there like sickness of heart.

The lover's ailment is different from all ailments;
Love is the astrolabe of God's mysteries.

'Sickness of heart' is also a main theme of much of Urdu poetry. And none other than Aunty Munni Begum expressed it best. I indulged my passion for *ghazals* by constantly listening to her. When she sings, 'complications at every step, confusion for every soul'—'*har qadam zehmatian, har nafs uljhanain*', she is, actually, talking to me! I wondered at her mystical habit of popping up at fateful junctures of our lives! Whenever I hear her, I am transported to somewhere balanced and sublime.

My repeated hounding of the university bureaucracy eventually paid off. I returned to London a week or so before the anticipated delivery date. We waited anxiously. She was late. Saliha was amused, as were my parents, that I was convinced it was a girl. But one day I just could not wait any longer. '*Challo*', I suggested to my wife, let's go to the hospital. She was reluctant. 'It's not time yet', she said. 'We will go when I am good and ready'. She was ten days overdue. Ready or not, we were going to the hospital. She agreed to go, and I gently guided her towards St. Mary's Hospital, Paddington, which was then located only five minutes' walk from my parents' flat (in 1986, it relocated to its current position in Praed Street).

It was eight in the evening. By the time we reached the hospital gate, her contractions had started. She was immediately admitted to the labour ward. I asked the doctor on duty to let me stay with my wife. She agreed. Then I pushed a little: 'I would like to deliver the baby'. She looked at me in astonishment. The conversation that followed, I vaguely recall, went as follows.

'I am the father. I want to deliver my child'.

'We are obstetricians. Delivering babies is what *we* do'.

'As a father, I have a right'.

'You have the right to stand at a distance and watch'.

'Not good enough. I want to be involved in the actual delivery'.

'No, no. You know nothing about delivering babies'.

'I *do*. I am science journalist'.

'Who do you write for?'

'For *Nature*. The most foremost science journal in the world'.

The golden word had been uttered. *Nature*. The young obstetrician was also a budding researcher who was having problems in getting her papers published. So we reached a compromise: I will help with the publication of her paper, she will allow me to handle the baby just after the second stage of birth (she never contacted me, and the promise remained unfulfilled).

So it happened. I stood outside the booth watching the delivery. Then I was allowed inside and permitted to carry the baby just before the arrival of the placenta. As I had wished and always thought, it was a girl. This was when I made my first blunder, a categorical mistake for which Saliha never forgave me. An error of fatherly love. I kept hold of the baby. While she lay on the hospital bed, exhausted, with her arms stretched out for her child to be handed to her to hold and caress, I kept the baby in my arms. She had to be wrenched from me and handed to her mother.

She brought us great joy and changed the dynamics of family life. I wasn't going to be separated from both my wife and my daughter. A few months later, I quit my job at the Hajj Research Centre and brought all the money I had saved while working in Jeddah in a carrier bag (we were not allowed to open a bank account) to London. It was enough to buy a house. We moved out from our parent's place and moved into a modest dwelling in Colindale. It was to become our permanent home.

Life was hard. I managed to get a job as deputy editor of *Arabia: Islamic World Review* (now defunct), but it only lasted a few months. I got sacked for co-authoring an editorial that painted the then Saudi monarch, King Fahd bin Abdulaziz bin Saud, in a less than favourable light. I started working for *New Scientist*, but the income was never enough. Moreover, to Saliha's irritation, I was frequently on assignment in the Middle East. Or on research trips. Or attending a conference. At home, our lives revolved around Maha, Munni Begum and our cat, Lucy. I took Maha with me whenever and wherever I could. My nickname for her was '*Dunya*', my world, and she was the axis of my world; she *is* the axis of my world.

Our financial situation improved when I joined London Weekend Television (LWT) as a reporter. Conventional 16 mm film was being replaced with video, and my reports were shot on tapes (then referred to as ENG, electronic news gathering). The rough footage had to be edited. So almost every week, I would go down, tapes in hand, to the editing suites to have my reports edited and ready for transmission. The editor assigned to me was called Arun Kalarya. Our love of film, Indian culture and the fact that we spoke to each other in Urdu/Hindi/Punjabi was the superglue that bonded our friendship. It just so happened that Arun also lived in Colindale—just a few streets away from our house. So we met frequently, not just at work but also at our homes. Arun's wife, Indu, and Saliha connected instantly. They were of the same age, had the same effervescent personalities and behaved like sisters cemented together at birth. Indu was Saliha's confidant: my shortcomings as a husband (which were many, and emerging), were relayed to Indu in hushed tones. In times of trouble, Indu would be in our house within minutes.

An established tradition in our family requires that some of our closest friends must be Hindu/Jain. My father's best friend was Mr Mittal, who lived close to us when we lived in Hackney. Every Saturday morning, he would come to our house, the two friends would talk and laugh, and regale each other in the evening at the regular poetry recitals. My mother's best buddy was Surita, who lived next door but one when we lived in Amberley Estate. There was a constant flow of food to and fro. *Bhaturas* from Surita. *Bhindi* from ours. Children were constantly in each other's houses. So it was only natural for Saliha and Indu to form a lifelong, indestructible bond—they were 'besties'. Much as in my mother's house, our friends were a microcosm of the subcontinent—before it was divided. As my father used to say: 'there is no partition here'.

Shortly after I joined LWT, our son Zaid was born. I was a devoted husband during Saliha's pregnancy. I maintained a calendar of prenatal visits, and accompanied her to all the appointments. Unfortunately, I wasn't there at the crucial moment of birth. I was on assignment filming a report on racism against Asian doctors. This was my second categorical mistake: an error of a jobbing reporter. Saliha saw that as a lack of devotion. 'There was a twinkle in her eye', says Indu, when she held Zaid for the first time. She was exceptionally proud. A photo of the proud mother holding a few hours old Zaid adorns our house. There was a great deal of joy and happiness in our home. We had a little celebration when Saliha became a naturalised British citizen in July 1984.

One day, we were doing our weekly shopping at Sainsbury's, the local supermarket. Saliha leading from the front, examining every item for undesirable *haram* ingredients as well as price, pushing Zaid in his pram and me lagging behind holding Maha's hand. A young Asian woman recognised me, came over and embraced me without a hint of hesitation. 'You are the reporter from Eastern Eye', she exclaimed. Saliha's face turned red. When the woman left, Saliha turned around and snapped: 'me or television?' 'You', I replied, with a smile.

5

It was not easy for me to give up television. I was working hard but also enjoying myself. I was destined to be a star as one of the TV executives once told me. Being recognised on the street gives you something akin to a sugar rush. It also does something to your soul. Your self, '*nafs ammarah bi-su*', urges you to move away from what you understand as virtues and towards their debasing counterparts. The movement is subtle, but definite. I became arrogant (even more than my usual quota) and boastful. Too full of myself. I was not ready to give up my nascent television career just yet.

I often left home early and came back late. She felt neglected. First, she accused me of paying more attention to the children than her. I pleaded guilty. Then, she even accused me of paying more attention to Lucy, our cat, than her. This time I pleaded not guilty. One day, Saliha pronounced: 'I want another child'. I wasn't keen. 'Two are enough', I replied. She looked a bit despondent, but I thought nothing of it. A few weeks later, she asked: 'why are you being mean? Why can't we have another child?' I explained, we are just about coping with two. Think of all the multiple problems we will have with schools, universities, marriages. We took our children everywhere with us. I wanted to travel and write travel books and lugging three children around would be a burden too far. In any case, I pointed out, the population of the world is increasing too fast. Better to have fewer children for the sake of the planet. She was not convinced but said nothing.

The question emerged again a few weeks later. *Why can't we have another child?* This time I lost my temper. 'We can't, ok', I shouted at her. 'Stop asking'. She kept quiet, but that evening moved out of our bed into the small guest room. That was my third and most serious categorical mistake. An error of conceited modernity. I failed to realise that the lives of traditional women revolve around children. A home is not a home unless it is spotless and orderly (ours always was) and full of children running around destroying the created order, making mess everywhere. Two just won't do. Saliha's parents had five. Her grandparents had eight or nine. Ditto other relatives.

She said nothing. She didn't speak to me—at all. Like an idealised housewife, she would do all the chores perfectly. As soon as I returned from work, she would retire to her room, leaving me to have dinner alone or play with the children. All my attempts at cajoling failed. She would not utter a single word. This went on for days, then weeks, then months. Eventually, I too stopped trying to talk to her. We were like two strangers in a home. Then, she packed her bags and left for Pakistan, leaving me with the children.

I was confused. Was she suffering from postpartum depression, feeling sad and anxious after she had given birth to Zaid? Was she leaving me? The demands of the job at LWT were also taking their toll on me. It was not easy to look after two kids while trying to file reports and features for a demanding television programme.

I had a regular crew that accompanied me on shoots: director, cameraman (in those days they were all men), sound person, sparks (electricians) and production assistants (who kept the whole lot together and made sure we were at the right place at the right time). Sometimes the director would be replaced by a female assistant director. The director and I were very chummy and often mocked each other: he referred to me as 'the luminary' and I called him 'Mr Morgan', after the self-admitted dreamer of the 1966 film, *Morgan: A Suitable Case for Treatment*. But I was rather close to the assistant director. We often found ourselves together on long shoots, or working late at night. Her goal in life was to turn the romantic novels of the French playwright and novelist Francoise Sagan into mini-series for television, which she would direct. She wanted me to write the screenplays. I saw it as a challenge and was eager to try my hand at a different kind of writing than I was used to. I was trying to balance work with looking after two children, while trying to write a script till late at night. She volunteered to help with looking after the children, which I readily accepted. And, for a period, she moved into our house. We worked together on Sagan's first 1944 novel, which Sagan wrote while only eighteen, called *Bonjour Tristesse* (Hello Sadness).

Saliha returned after six months in Pakistan. Still silent. The only person she talked to was Indu. One evening I returned after a long day of editing to find my collection of tapes and newly acquired CDs all over the living room floor. I thought the children had been up to their usual naughtiness. But then I heard a familiar sound. I rushed upstairs to the main bedroom and found Saliha sitting on *our* bed, crying. My portable cassette player was by her side. The tape was playing Munni Begum:

> *Bewafa se bhi pyar hota hai*
> You can even love the unfaithful
> *Yaar kuch bhi ho yaar hota hai*
> Friends are friends whatever they are
> *Saath mein uske hai raqeeb toh kya*
> So what if my fate is tied to him
> *Phool ke saath kaante hota hai*
> Even flowers have thorns with them.
> *Jab woh aate nahi shabe waada*
> When he doesn't return on promised nights
> *Maut ka intazaar hota hai*
> I wait for my death.

She broke her long silence when she saw me. 'I love you *jani*', she sobbed. 'I can't live without you'. She opened her arms, and I rushed to embrace her. 'You are going to...' She could not get the words out of her mouth. 'I want...' I put my hands gently on her mouth. 'You don't have to say anything', I murmured. 'I am not going anywhere'. I changed the tape in the cassette player to another Munni Begum *ghazal*: *Ek Bar Muskura Do*

Paradise will swing,
The atmosphere will smile,
If you smile,
God will smile.
Smile once (again).

Two months later, she informed me that there was a thin blue line. Our third child, Zain, was born seven months later.

Once again, I was not there at the crucial time. By now I had quit LWT and started to work for East–West University in Chicago. My first task there was to organise a major international conference on '*Dawa* and Development'. When Zain was born, I was in Mecca running the conference. But I was able to talk to Saliha immediately after the birth and that was a consolation—a last-minute goal. I think Indu organised the 'long-distance call' as they used to be called in the 1980s. My friend, and the children's godmother, Merryl Wyn Davies, who was about to join me in Mecca, drove her to the hospital. The two women had some warm words with the proud mother. When Merryl joined me in Mecca, we jumped up and down in joy and had a glass or two of 'Jeddah Champagne' (orange juice and soda water) in celebration.

The first few years after the arrival of Zain were difficult. He was born with his feet facing inwards and had to have a string of operations to have them corrected. There were numerous visits to the hospital and to see the consultant, who was called 'Mr Angel'. Saliha used to say, 'Zain arrived with a *farishta* (angel) in tow'. The boy had his feet in plaster for months. He would hobble around the house damaging and breaking things with plastered feet which had the gravity of a small boulder. Even as he grew older, not much changed. He had inherited the family trait of clumsiness.

By now, our modest dwelling in Colindale had become sizeable. As the children arrived, we turned the garage into a room, added another with an extension, then transformed the attic into a study, and finally added a conservatory. The children attended the local primary school. I left East–West University to work, along with Merryl, in Malaysia with my friend Anwar Ibrahim, who then held a number of ministerial portfolios, and commuted between London and Kuala Lumpur—often with wife and children who instantly fell in love with the country. It was a joyous time with a great deal of travel within Malaysia—we spent a memorable few days in a tree house in the National Park trying to see a tapir without success. There were 'intellectual discourses' in Kuala Lumpur, where local, regional, international and Islamic issues of the period were analysed. It was also a prolific period for me as a writer. I did most of my writing in London, cooped up in the attic where I was seldom disturbed. I only came down when Saliha would shout, from the kitchen: 'Zia, lunch!', 'Zia, tea' and 'Zia, dinner'.

Life changed a gear when it was time for the children to attend secondary school. And Saliha had had enough of being a housewife. Now she wanted to work.

6

Most of our arguments were centred around the children—how we should bring them up, how they should play, what school they should go to, what they should study at university. Saliha wanted her children to grow up with a strong sense of right and wrong, good and bad, virtue and vice. They could not be left to their own devices and had to be told what they should, ought and must do. I wanted my children to be people with imagination, perception, observation and reasoning, which I thought they possessed by virtue of being children. I also thought they would develop a sense of right and wrong as they grew. So there was always a tug of war. But somehow, we reached a middle ground. Dolls with the entire package of adult pornography (with big breasts, slender waist and long legs) were out. But Maha could play with more locally made 'halal dolls', made of cotton or wood, that I bought back from my travels. In general, modern toys were out—such as Teletubbies, Hollywood-inspired nonsense and Playstations—but toys that involved building, thinking and creative play were allowed, such as modelling clay, wooden blocks and jigsaw puzzles. Television was restricted, but kids could watch what the parents were watching. This was easy for Saliha as she almost exclusively watched Pakistani television dramas and Bollywood films. But rather difficult for me as I watched Hollywood and foreign films. Pop music was discouraged, but Bollywood singing and dancing was accepted. Most of all, however, reading was promoted at every opportunity. The children usually received books for their birthday presents.

When it came to schools, there was no way Saliha would allow Maha to attend a mixed, co-ed establishment. Fortunately, there was a reasonably good girls' school not too far from our place. She toyed with the idea of sending Zaid to a private school. There was a famous and highly recommended one relatively close. We couldn't afford the astronomical fees. But we had Zaid sit the entrance examination anyway. He passed with flying colours. We used the result to get him admitted to the most sought-after boys' school in our borough. She wanted Zain to go to an Islamic school, but accepted my suggestion of a Catholic alternative. It took some effort and threats involving letters from the Vatican, which both Saliha and I visited that year and where I had contacts, to get him admitted. The daily school runs were a nightmare as the three schools were in three different locations. Saliha dropped the children off in the morning. I collected them in the afternoon. Sometimes. Other times, she took it all on her shoulders.

She was happy when I and Merryl gently ushered Maha towards law. We got her interested by sitting with her to watch endless episodes of *LA Law*. Zaid liked building things so it was natural for him to study engineering. But we had a long running battle with Zain. I wanted him to study philosophy and got him interested at a young age by reading Plato—we began with *Symposium* and went on to *The*

Republic. She was incensed. 'What good would that do?', she demanded to know. 'What kind of job will he get as a philosopher?' No answer would satisfy her. The battle raged for years and became worse when Zain decided to attend the University of Kent, which meant he had to leave home. It took long, protracted negotiations before she reluctantly agreed to allow her youngest child to leave home to pursue university education outside London. But she wasn't happy. And she made that clear.

With the children at various universities, she had more time on her hands. She wasn't satisfied by just being a housewife. She wanted to work, and there was only one job she wanted to do. To work with children. She had an infinite love for children. Not just her children, but children *per se*. Not just in her household, where she was Begum, but everywhere. She would use the Urdu word *bacha*—child— when talking to her own kids, even when they were mature adults. 'When I start work', she asserted, 'what I earn is mine. You have no right over it'. I agreed. 'And what I earn is also yours', I teased. 'I already know *that*', she shot back.

During September 1980, she started to work part time at the village school, a short drive from our house. It caters for children from three to nineteen, with special or complex needs or disabilities. Some are on the autistic spectrum, but most have severe and profound needs relating to disorders such as cerebral palsy, Down's syndrome, cystic fibrosis and disorders of movement and coordination. For her, it was not so much 'work' as a cherished vocation. That's just what she always wanted to do: to care for special needs children. When she started to work full-time, she undertook a string of courses and training programmes: health and social care, multi-sensory cues training, manual handling in a care environment, life support, risk assessment, musculoskeletal injury, supporting complex needs, infection prevention and control, the moving and handling of specialised equipment (such as hoists) and food allergy awareness. With all these she had no problem. But when it came to such things as legislation and 'Diploma in Team Leading', she sought the help of her family. We all ran in different directions. 'Please, I need help with this', she would plead. Eventually, Maha or I would sit with her and see her through the course.

I agreed to help her on a particular course on organisation management. We went through various sections of the course. The first section was on vision. She learned that a 'vision is an image of the future that an organisation wants to achieve in the future'. I asked: what is your vision? 'I envisage', she replied, 'playing with and looking after my grandchildren in the future'. The second section was on mission. We were told: 'mission is the goal an organisation sets itself in answers to such questions as what, how and why we do what we do and who are we doing it for'. What is your mission in life? I playfully asked Saliha. 'My mission', she replied without a second for thought, 'is to get my children married as soon as possible so I can have grandchildren'. The course went on to strategy, objectives and targets. 'My target is to get the boys married within a year'. The boys had their own ideas.

She worked at the village school for over forty years and never missed a single day. She would go to work even when she was not feeling too well. 'My children need me', she would say. Her love was reciprocated: her pupils as well as her colleagues adored her. Every now and then, her colleagues would come after school, or at weekends, for tea. Our living room would witness lively conversation and laughter, which would reverberate all the way to the attic, where I would be working.

Just before her fortieth birthday, Saliha complained of a stomach ache. I suggested she should go and see our GP. But she was reluctant; she just did not like the idea of seeing a doctor. The pain continued. One night it was obvious that she was in considerable pain, and I could not contain myself. 'We are going to the hospital', I asserted. 'No, no', she squeaked. But I wasn't going to take no for an answer. I took her to the Northwick General Hospital. We waited for about three hours before she was seen. The A&E doctor sent her for an X-ray. We sat for another four hours, and it became obvious that she wasn't going to have an X-ray any time soon. By now, it was early morning and we were exhausted. 'Enough of this shit', I bellowed. 'We will go private'. We drove to a private hospital not too far from where we live. But before we could reach the entrance we were stopped by some firemen. 'Turn back, turn back', they shouted. The hospital was on fire. 'You see', Saliha snapped. 'God does not want me to see a doctor'. 'He does', I replied, as I reversed and drove towards another private hospital some distance away. She was immediately seen by a specialist who diagnosed cholecystitis—inflammation of the gallbladder. He prescribed a cocktail of medicines which worked.

On Saturday 31 January 1998, we celebrated with some fanfare the joint fortieth birthdays (a couple of days late) of Saliha and Indu. The celebrations were held at Indu's house, where families and friends of the bosom companions gathered. There were tributes, speeches and much Bollywood dancing. Hamida and Merryl were present and in top form. Zafar and Sameena, who by then had moved to Chicago, came for the birthday. Sameena had written a poem for the occasion, which she read in her amiable style.

Saliha

You've turned the big four O
All these years you maintained a glow

My first recollection of you
A hurried introduction at Heathrow
Simply dressed in black and white
With an obedient smile

You began your life with Zia, Jeddah bound
Soon that turned your world around

In contrast to your serene self
Zia was wrapped, only in himself

All these years…past
Quietly you've won…at last
Children, home, cat and all
Love, affection and patient stand tall

Your friendship I truly treasure
Twenty years of real pleasure

Hats off to you
Now, that's my view.

7

Sameena was right. I tended to be wrapped up in myself. I suspect that most writers are. I needed time and space to write and had to travel for research. But Saliha came to appreciate this. When people asked me how you have managed to write so many books, I always replied: it's thanks to my supporting wife. In one respect, she is the invisible but ever-present co-author of all my works, much more than a muse. She actually features in a few. When someone visited our house, she would point, with a beaming smile on her face, to the bookshelf that held most of my titles: 'my husband wrote these'. However, she seldom agreed with what I had to say.

She loved to travel, but only with me. The only place she would travel to on her own was Pakistan. She visited her family there quite regularly, whenever she got a break from work. Elsewhere, we travelled together—to Malaysia, Singapore, Turkey, Spain, Saudi Arabia, the UAE, Bosnia-Herzegovina, Sweden, France, Morocco, Egypt and Tunisia. We spent quite a lot of time in some of these places—and revisited them, again and again. But Saliha preferred to go to new places every time. 'We have already been there', she would complain, 'let's go somewhere new'. 'Like where', I would reply in annoyance, 'the North Pole?' I would save money for her to spend on trips. It would be handed to her when we reached our destination. 'Here', I would say, 'some bread for your delectation'. She would take the money, wander around shops and bazars all day, pulling me here, pushing me there. And at the end of the gruelling day, hand all the money back. She liked everything she saw. Never bought anything she saw. Unless she was with her daughter, who is a spendthrift.

The last twenty years of my life with Saliha developed into joyful sets of choreographed routines. We had worked out what we needed and what made us happy. She would leave for work in the morning. I would have my constitutional coffee and work till one o'clock and then come down from the attic for lunch. The days when she used to call out 'Zia, lunch' had long gone. I had to make my own lunch and then get back to work. She would return near four o'clock by which time I had to have her tea and biscuits (usually, one McVitie's digestive, one Jaffa cake) prepared. As soon as she opened the door, she would shout: 'Is my *chai* ready?' We would have tea together. I would return to the attic. She would watch some Pakistani news channel till six and then prepare the dinner. Around seven, I had to come down for dinner as soon as she called. The meal could not be allowed to get cold. We would dine together while watching the Channel 4 News.

Thorny issues raised their head after dinner. Saliha had established two strict rules that had to be followed or, as the proverb has it, hell hath no fury. First rule: Islam and Pakistan were above criticism. Criticism of these subjects were to be limited to my books and not made in front of her. If I made a comment on some story on Pakistan that we had watched on the news, it would be taken as a vile calumny, even if well intentioned, on the sanctity of the Land of the Pure. As far as Islam was concerned, I had better keep my mouth shut—something that was practically impossible for me. One afternoon, I was watching a Pakistani news channel with her at teatime. The host was interviewing the late famous singer, Junaid Jamshed, who gave up a highly successful career in pop music, grew a preposterous beard and became a missionary. The host asked the singer: what do you love most about Pakistan? Jamshed replied: 'the devotion of the people to Islam. Pakistanis are fervent in prayer and rush to their mosques as soon as the *azan* is called', he said. During Friday prayers, he pointed out, the mosques are full to the brim. Pakistanis are very observant of Ramadan. Et cetera. The interview ended with the suggestion that God was looking favourably towards Pakistan and its people.

I just could not contain myself and burst into laughter. Saliha saw this as a double whammy: not only had I laughed at Pakistan, I had also somehow denigrated Islam. She was incensed. 'Begum', I tried to explain. 'Think about it. If God was showering his blessings on Pakistan the country would not be in a complete and utter mess'. She frowned. So I went further. 'Consider that over 250 million Pakistanis have been fervently praying five times a day for over seventy years asking God to sort out their country. But no reply has been forthcoming. So, there are only three possibilities. One: God doesn't exist. Two: He is not listening to Pakistanis. Three: if He is listening, His answer is no. Get lost you rotten sods'. She dismissed my analysis. She had her own critical take on Islam, which was idealism peppered with hope and wrapped in tradition. She moved out of our bed for three days—the specified *fiqhi* time for being angry!

Second rule: films and television shows containing sex and violence were totally forbidden. As a news junkie, I would proceed from Channel 4 News to Sky News at eight, BBC News at nine, ITN News at 10 and end the evening with Newsnight or Press Review. Saliha saw this as demented. After dinner, she would get her iPad out, put on her headphones and watch Pakistani dramas and comedy shows. On selected days, we watched *Poirot* or *Murder in*

Paradise together, programmes where the murder takes place off stage and no sex is involved. She also liked *Bake Off* and other cooking shows and *Doc Martin*. We usually sat at the opposite end of the sofa, engaged in our chosen activity. But there was a sublime connection: we kept an eye on each other, sometimes leaning sideways to hold hands when no one was around. When I was watching something that was not on the approved list, or a sex scene or violence appeared on screen, she would mutter, without moving her gaze from her iPad, 'change the channel, change the channel', or 'fast forward, fast forward'. If I was watching something tragic, howls of laughter would be coming from her side as she watched a Pakistani comedy. Watching something like *Game of Thrones*, where sex and violence are the order of the day, was well-nigh impossible. '*Astaghfirullah!*' (I seek forgiveness from Allah) she would exclaim, without lifting her eyes from the iPad, followed by a very loud: '*Auzubillah Minashaitan Nirajeem*' (I seek refuge from Allah from the accursed Shaitan). That was a signal for me to switch off, while she continued to regale herself with whatever she was watching.

Sometimes however, I would not concede defeat. I had a trump card up my sleeve: 'Coke Studio', the truly brilliant, and long running, Pakistani music show. Its strength lies in its synthesis of traditional and classical music—*ghazals*, *qawwali*, folk and Sufi—with contemporary rock and pop. I would turn to YouTube and start listening to the latest season. She would slowly raise her eyes from the iPad and then put it down. She knew that I had pulled a fast one. We would both become immersed, mesmerised. Just to annoy her a little, I would play a particular *ghazal* that I really liked again and again, savouring the words, looking for metaphorical connections. The only time I got her to abandon her iPad completely was when we watched all 448 episodes of the Turkish show *Ertugrul: Resurrection* on Netflix. Indeed, the whole family watched it together. No one was allowed to watch ahead on their own. Here the problems I usually faced with Saliha were reversed. The show, which revolves around the exploits of the father of the first Ottoman caliph Osman Ghazi, is full of endless sword fights, numerous elaborate marriage ceremonies and sermons on Islam. Now it was me saying, 'fast forward, fast forward'. But Saliha wanted to watch every second. Even the violence didn't bother her.

We had a division of labour. She had this strange ability to instantly pick out that one damn thing you'd missed. If I spent all day painting a room, for example, she would walk in and immediately point to the square inch that had escaped. It was perhaps her most annoying ability. Consequently, I was not allowed to wash the dishes or clean the house as, inevitably, I did a bad job. So I did the gardening, which I loved. On the whole, she approved. Every spring, when I brought the garden back to life, she would make a video and send it to the extended family: 'this

is our garden'. But there had to be an issue. So it became: Saliha versus weeds. I couldn't be bothered with sorting out the weeds on the paved areas of our front and back gardens. She could not stand them. There would be determined and protracted battles between the two adversaries. She would pour weed killer on them, but they would return reinvigorated in a few days. She would meticulously rake them out, but the blighters would come back as soon as she had finished. I got her a device to burn them. That didn't help either. Finally, we got an electric weed remover that seemed to do the job. But it was chargeable. So the charge often ran out during the battle. It was a campaign she was destined to lose.

She never threw anything away. If anything could be used in some distant future, it had to be kept. The trouble was she had a very loose definition of what could be used, and it included boxes. All kind of boxes. Boxes which were used for her wedding jewellery. Perfume boxes (perfume finished decades ago!). Boxes for beauty products. Shoe boxes. Gift boxes. Cookie boxes. If something came in a box, the thing itself may or may not be used, but the box itself was kept for use in the future—which, of course, never arrived (the future has a habit of doing this). So boxes kept piling up—in cupboards, cabinets, up in the attic, down in the garage. Her side of the house was full of boxes. My side was briming with books. Books and boxes constantly fought each other for dominance and extra space.

She was always discreet. Never said a bad word about me, or expressed affection, in front of the children. But love was showered when we were alone in bed, along with all the complaints. We spoke in Urdu. She would laugh at my comments at gatherings. But at night: how could you say such and such, why did you mock him, why did you criticise that. I would offer no defence for the things I often said could not be defended as far as she was concerned. Anxieties about her children would be whispered. She had acquired the habit of repeating herself—especially when she thought her complaints were not being listened to or were ignored—so I would let her talk. She would give an endless list of my shortcomings.

Occasionally, she would complain about the injustices of the world, the suffering she saw every day on the news that she could no longer watch, the wars and destruction she could not endure. But she said it as though I was to blame for all these ills. I would exclaim in exhaustion: 'Why stop at violations of human rights? Why don't you also blame me for Nuclear Holocaust?' But it would all end with mutual expressions of undying love.

I thought she was the most pure and kind-hearted person God had created on earth. She was grateful for, as she wrote in her 'Moment's Journal' on 29 January 2018, 'having loving children and husband'.

Covid-19 arrived just over a year later. We spent two years huddled together, going out for occasional permitted walks. Saliha spent some time planning her retirement.

8

In early October 2022, Saliha complained of pain in her stomach. She went to her GP who fobbed her off with antibiotics. They didn't work. She went back: this time the GP organised an ultrasound and blood tests. She was then referred to a gynaecologist, who organised a CT scan on 17

October, followed by an MRCP on 25 and a PET scan on 31 October. During this time her pain continued to increase. She became jaundiced and started vomiting, had little or no appetite and lost five kilograms in weight. She was in acute agony. Maha took time off work to look after her as her symptoms became worse and worse. On 4 November, Maha, Zaid and Zain went with her to see a consultant at the Royal Free Hospital, Hampstead, in London. They were told that a biopsy confirmed gallbladder cancer—'an adenocarcinoma'. The treatment would be chemotherapy with the aim of disease control rather than eradication. But if the disease is confirmed as locally advanced and she has an excellent response to chemotherapy, other treatments could be used to expel the cancer.

I was unaware of all this.

An election was on the horizon in Kuala Lumpur. And I was working on Anwar's campaign. I would ring Saliha every other day. But she never told me anything was wrong. 'I am fine. Don't worry about me', she would say. 'Just make sure Anwar wins the election'. A week after her diagnosis, I was in Tambun, the major town of the Kinta District in Perak, the seat Anwar was contesting. There was small doubt that he would win the seat. So, I went there with my colleagues to judge the situation, a couple of days before Anwar was due to arrive in the town to launch his campaign. I went to the airport to meet him and communicate what I thought he should push at the hustings. But before I could say anything, he shook my hand, and pulled me near him. 'Has Maha rung you', he asked. 'No', I replied. 'She has something important to tell you'.

I became concerned. I rang Maha immediately. 'I can't talk now', she told me. 'But *we* will ring you in the evening'. The *we* increased my anxiety.

That evening there was a meeting in Anwar's suite at his hotel. The entire election team of some thirty people were there. I was sitting next to Anwar when Maha rang. He asked me to take the call in his bedroom.

'Zaid, Zain and Mum are here', Maha said. 'And Zaid needs to talk to you', she handed the phone to her brother. 'We have something important to tell you', Zaid said. There was a long pause. 'Mum has gallbladder cancer'. He could hardly get the words out of his mouth.

I was stunned. 'What, what?', I mumbled. Another long silence. Then I became angry. 'What has happened to my wife? Why did you not tell me earlier?' I started sobbing.

Maha came to the phone. 'Mum did not want us to tell you. She did not want you to worry. She wants you to concentrate on your work'.

'I will leave immediately', I exclaimed. 'I will be with you by tomorrow evening'. 'Let me speak to her'.

Maha gave her mobile to Saliha. 'I did not want to worry you', she said. 'And I don't want you to worry. I will be alright'. She paused. 'And there is no need to for you to come back immediately. Stay there till the election, till Anwar becomes the prime minister. You have waited a long time for that'.

So typical, I thought. Even in her darkest hour she is concerned about me rather than herself.

Both Saliha and Maha insisted that I stay and continue my work in Kuala Lumpur. Saliha's chemotherapy was supposed to begin on 15 November, and I could return the day after the election. I agreed reluctantly. But I was angry that Anwar knew, my sister and other members of family had been told. But I knew not.

A week later, Maha rang in panic. It was the middle of the night in London. 'Mum is vomiting continuously', she sobbed. 'I can't cope. Come now'. I took the first flight out of Kuala Lumpur.

I arrived early in the morning and ran straight to the bedroom. Saliha and Maha were sleeping together. They got up when they saw me. I ran to embrace my wife. I could not believe her transformation: she had been reduced to a skeleton; her face was pale. She was unable to eat for days. Yet, she was composed. I held her in my arms for several minutes, sobbing. 'We need to take her to hospital—*Now*!', I asserted. Saliha was reluctant. 'I hate hospitals', she said. But we took her anyway.

On 10 November, she was kept in the hospital for a night. A procedure was performed to sort out her severe constipation. She was given medicine to stop her vomiting. And we brought her back home the following day. She felt and looked much better and was very happy to see my sister, Huma, who had arrived from California that day. We anxiously waited for her chemotherapy to start.

I took her to the Royal Free Hospital in Hampstead, London, on 15 November when her chemotherapy sessions were to begin. But it was not to be. She was too malnourished. The bilirubin levels in her blood were too high. The first part of her small intestines (duodenal) was totally blocked. She was immediately admitted. A week later, she was taken to the theatre to have a stent inserted in her bile duct. The procedure went horribly wrong. It was done using local anaesthetic, so she was conscious throughout and heard the surgeons talking. 'It's not working'. 'Too much fluid'. 'I can't' get to it'. 'She's is losing a lot of blood'. Saliha came out of the theatre terrified and upset. 'I don't want this. I don't want this', she kept saying. I consoled her; and it took a while for her to unruffle.

Later that day, when she had returned to her ward, she was in a great deal of pain. 'I can't imagine your pain', I grieved. 'No you can't', she replied. 'Only those with pain know what it is like to suffer'. She thought for a while, then she said: 'Jani, I don't want to be a burden on my children'. Then she prayed: '*Ya Allah*, don't turn me into a burden for my husband and children'. No, no, I said. 'Begum: you are the centrifugal force of our lives. Our lives revolve around you. You can never be a burden on us. Please don't have such thoughts'. She smiled, turned over, and tried to go to sleep.

A second attempt was made a week later. This time a senior surgeon was called. Two stents were simultaneously inserted in the bile duct. The procedure went well. It was the day of the 15th General Election in Malaysia. I was kept posted during that stressful night. But no one had conclusively won the election. We could say it was a hung parliament. Saliha remained in hospital. Meanwhile, five agonising days later, Anwar was sworn in as the tenth prime minister of Malaysia. Things seemed to be looking up.

We visited her daily. The kids. My sister. Her friends and colleagues also came to see her. She seemed happiest when her friend Indu and when her colleagues from the school came to see her. I got jealous. 'You seemed happier to see them than me', I complained. 'You are my husband', Saliha replied. 'You are naturally bound to me. You have to be with me. You can do nothing else. You and I have no free will. We are bound together in eternal love'. She paused to adjust her intravenous drips. 'They are my friends and colleagues. They have their free will intact. They don't have to visit me. Yet they come. So I am happier to see that they too love me'.

After two weeks, she returned from the hospital feeling much better. She started to eat. Albeit mostly liquids, and slowly. Her vomiting had stopped. Although she was still having problems with constipation. We saw her consultant on 9 December. We were told that she was very happy with Saliha's progress; her bile duct issue was 'now almost completely resolved'. Her first chemotherapy went well, and three weeks later, the second was even better. The cancer nurse rang to say that she had made 'remarkable progress'. It was all very encouraging. We felt relieved, and admired the courage that my Begum had shown during this tough period.

My sister felt confident enough to return to California. Her departure coincided with the arrival of my niece, Hana. Indu was a daily visitor. And her colleagues too came to see her regularly. She was so happy. And on her way to a semblance of recovery.

On 17 January she had her third session of chemotherapy. By all accounts it went well. But she couldn't sleep the following two nights. She was severely constipated and the vomiting returned.

On the morning of 20 January, she looked pale and unwell. We thought she needed another procedure to relieve her constipation. She was not keen to go yet again to the hospital. But we thought, and assured her, that she would only be there for a night. After all the treatment was going reasonably well. 'You will be back by tomorrow, once the procedure is done', I said. Maha had a work-related matter to attend, and I suggested she should go. She had taken enough days off work. I wanted to take her to the hospital, but Zaid said he would take his mum and look after her. 'You stay home and rest', he said. 'I will keep you posted'. 'I will come and see you in the evening as soon as the tests are done and you have been admitted', I said. Maha and I hugged her as she left with Zaid at 11 am.

At one o'clock, Zaid rang to say that she would have a blood transfusion. A couple of hours later, he informed me that she was going for a scan. At around five o'clock he rang again. His voice was shaking. 'Dad', he murmured, 'Mum. She is very poorly'.

I dropped everything, called an Uber. I wanted the driver to get me to the hospital as fast as he could. But he took his time and insisted on telling me his life story.

When I got to the hospital, I ran straight to the emergency ward. A nurse took me to Saliha's bed.

Zaid was standing next to her weeping. I saw my beloved lying on a stretcher motionless. For a minute or two, I was totally paralysed. I couldn't speak. Then, I shouted: 'What happened?' 'My wife is dead? How could that be?' I held her hand. I stroked her face. I kissed her cheeks. 'Saliha! Saliha! Saliha! My Saliha'. I had no control of myself. I could not look at her in that state. I ran out of the ward and into the hospital compound. I was howling. I rang Maha. 'Your mum, your mum has died'. There was loud scream at the other end. Then the phone went silent. I rang Zain: 'Our world has collapsed. Your ma has passed away'. I rang my brother. I rang Indu. All the while I was inconsolable. I was in shock. Disorientated. Despondent. Highly distressed. I walked up and down, round and round, in front of the hospital. And started attracting undue attention from the passers-by. Eventually, I ran back to the ward.

I paced nervously in front of Saliha. I kept stroking her hand. Kissing her on her cheeks. While trying to regain control of myself. Soon Zain arrived and stood motionless in front of his mother, next to his brother. Bewildered. Confused. Then, a hospital chaplain—an imam—arrived and began to recite the Qur'an. That had some calming influence on us all. Then he prayed for Saliha to be forgiven. My insides exploded. 'Forgiven? What is there to be forgiven', I bellowed. 'How can God forgive when there is nothing to forgive?' It is I, her husband, her *jani*, I thought, who needs forgiveness. 'Saliha, my Saliha, please forgive me'. 'Please forgive me'. *Mere jan mujay maaf karu*. My Begum, forgive me for all my categorical mistakes, for everything'.

The junior doctor on duty took me and Zaid to a secluded part of the ward. 'My sincere condolences', he mumbled. 'We were waiting for the results of her scan', he continued, 'when her gallbladder ruptured. We did everything we could. The cancer had spread all over her body'. He handed us a 'document'—a printed sheet which stated the time of death: 18.11. Just a few minutes before I arrived. I asked Zaid if she had said anything to him. 'Yes dad', he replied. 'She said make sure you ask the doctor if my cancer is in recession'. She wanted to live. And she had so much to live for.

I looked around, and there was no Maha. She was on her way to the hospital, devastated with grief. I had to see her first. I ran out of the hospital and waited outside the A&E entrance. She arrived in a taxi within a few minutes. She was wailing. I put my arms around her and held her tightly. I walked slowly towards the ward, all the time with a firm grip around Maha, while trying to console her. But she continued to scream 'mum, mum'. By the time we entered the ward, her screams had become quite loud. A female nurse came, blocked our way, and threatened to call security if Maha did not calm down. 'Get out of my way', Maha shouted. 'How dare you stop me from going to my mother'. A male nurse rushed towards us. He was from a Middle Eastern background, and seemed to understand our grief. He pushed the female nurse aside, and escorted us to Saliha.

We were soon joined by my brother, his wife, Farah, and daughter, and Indu, and sons Ashis and Anish. Everyone in disbelief, and in tears.

Our grief had now grown exponentially and flooded our entire being. I was drenched in tears. Maha sobbed uncontrollably. Zaid wept incessantly. Zain stood motionless, tears in his eyes, as though, for him, time had stopped. I felt as though my very being had disintegrated. My innards were only loosely attached to my body. They were falling off, bit by bit, and I was disintegrating into so many atoms and molecules. The glue that held me together had dissolved. Half of my self had gone. And the remaining half was falling apart.

Saliha's illness had been kept hidden from her mother—my *khala*. Now, she had to be told. It was not possible for me. When she was eventually told by her son, she rang me. '*Khala*', I sobbed, 'please forgive me. I could not look after your daughter. Khala, pray that Saliha forgives me. I let her down. I was not even there when she took her last breath. Please forgive me'. Crying ceaselessly, she replied: 'No Zia, *baitay*. It was the will of God. He will forgive us all'.

There was a huge crowd at her funeral. My niece, Hana, was the first to arrive with her family the day after Saliha died. Then my sister and nephew, Atif, who had returned one last time to see my Dulhan. Her school gave the day off to the staff to attend the funeral. My friends, her friends—we lost count. She was buried in Mill Hill cemetery, not far from where we live.

Over the next three or four weeks, messages and mails of sympathy poured in. There was a continuous flow of visitors who came to convey their condolences. Indu came almost every day, loaded with food. Saliha's colleagues visited us a number of times, encumbered with a string of dishes. My sister's friend, Sadia, came and went; and every time she returned with even more fare. There were many visitors we hardly knew. And a couple we did not know at all. They claimed that they had once met Saliha! The house was full of people—day and night.

Then, they stopped coming. My sister, niece and nephew went away. The house became empty.

The absence of Saliha was a mournful present. She turned the house into our home. Every corner of our home was touched by her style, charm and elegance. She was everywhere. But nowhere. I couldn't sleep at night and spent most of the days in tears. Every second, every moment, I longed for my Begum. I could not bear to be in the house without her. Eventually, I summoned the strength to go back to Malaysia, where Anwar Ibrahim was now prime minister, after three decades of our grinding struggles—all of which had been witnessed and shared by Saliha. Maha and Zaid decided to go with me. Zain wanted to be left alone. 'This is the most traumatic event of my life', he said. 'I need to be alone. I need to find my own way to overcome my grief'. While we flew to Kuala Lumpur, Zain went hiking.

9

Our house has a recognisable black door. For me, it is pregnant with expectation. I opened it with great joy. Wherever I went in the world, whenever I returned, I opened the door to a loving embrace. If it was too early in the morning, and she was still sleeping, she would murmur '*Aa Gai*'—you are back. If it was a little later, and she was getting ready to go to work, she would come and embrace me and say: 'your lunch is in the fridge'. If it was at night, I would just slip in bed beside her. She would turn around, embrace me, and whisper: 'I love you *jani*'.

But this time, after a few weeks in Kuala Lumpur, and a couple of months after her death, I returned and could not open the door. Our neighbour, Farhan, son of my Malaysian friend, Ahmad Nazri Abdullah, was leaving for work, along with his wife Sara. They said Salaam. Then, Sara remarked: 'Uncle, the weeds have taken over your front garden'. I hadn't noticed. All I saw was the door.

I stood in front of the door for several minutes, shaking. Tears rolled down my cheeks. The key dropped from my hand. As I bent to pick the key, the words of Omar Khayyam echoed in my head:

> There was a Door to which I found no key:
> There was a veil through which I could not see
> Some little talk awhile of Me and Thee
> There seemed - and then no more of Me and Thee.

It took a little while for me to compose myself. Eventually, I opened the door, and went inside the house. I threw my luggage in the doorway, and sat in the living room. The house was truly empty for the first time. She was not there; there was no '*Aa Gai*', no loving embrace, no murmurs of *jani*. I could hear nothing. I could see nothing. I yearned for her voice. I longed to see her radiant face. I felt a haunting sense of incompleteness—exposed, as though I had been skinned, my body was just bones and flesh without the protective layer of the skin. The protective layer was always at our home, the fulcrum of my life. That is where I found myself and my body united with my skin, my soul with my being. But our home for over forty years did not feel like a home. It was just a house. How can the body survive without the skin? How would I survive separated from my soulmate? There was an absence, an eternal absence that I could not bear. I wept uncontrollably. After some time, I managed to get up, climb the stairs to our bedroom, and throw myself on the bed.

I fell asleep, or rather drifted into a state of suspension, somewhere between asleep and being conscious of my surroundings. I heard a movement. I thought it was the rattling of internal doors, and ignored it. Moments later, I heard another rustling sound. Then I felt as though someone had sat at the end of the bed. I looked up in fear. But my fear evaporated instantly as I gazed at the serene face of my Begum. She was looking and smiling at me. My *Dhulan*, swathed in garments like the day she married me. But not in red. She was covered with a soft white blanket that my sister had brought for her when she was going through her cancer treatment. I got up to embrace her. As usual, at first she was reluctant, then she threw the blanket around me. The eternal absence transformed into a perpetual presence. I walked down to the living room, and then all over the house, with Saliha wrapped around me, as though she was a life-enhancing blanket. The two as one. A door was ajar. She turned my grief into grace. Even in death she was concerned about me. In life, she displayed a bundle of virtues to be emulated. She was my life. She *is* my life. *Meri Jaan.*

10

How fortunate I was to have her in my life. How unfortunate I am to lose her. Left with a longing that knows no bounds. What remains is just a name that was built over 64 years. Her birth certificate read simply Saliha Begum. The Pakistani passport of 1977 has Saliha Basit in blue, to which was added Sardar in black. Since then, she took the name as her own, no longer an afterthought. She expanded what meaning can be put in a name. Enriching our moral compass so that it may always point towards justice and compassion. Ensuring the Sardars would not be without virtue. She was Saliha Begum Basit Sardar.

In the distance, I can hear Munni Begum singing.

> I don't know how the evil eye
> Of the world fell upon me
> My nest is broken
> I sit in a gathering, head bowed
> Kill me, just kill me.

After

The three Begums died within three years, without realising their *tamanas, arzoos,* their cherished desires. For me, three losses, one after another, all rolled into one giant trauma. How do you cope with such cumulative bereavements?

You don't.

In Muslim circles, your relatives and friends would hug you and utter one single word: '*sabr*'. Have patience. But where does patience come from? How does one acquire it? Especially someone like me who has little patience to start with. What was it that Hamida said? 'You have so little patience that you came into the world three weeks early'. Patience is something you need to avoid making hasty decisions that you may regret later on. It is something you need for long queues, traffic jams, that irritating child who keeps watching noisy cartoons on his smart phone, to master an art you are clearly incapable of mastering. It is something you need for living people, to build and enhance a relationship, to tolerate people who in reality should not be tolerated. But how do you have patience for those who are not there?

You just cannot help missing them, try as hard as you can. In some fragmented moments, I get the urge to stop working, go down from the attic, and see what Hamida is up to. Only to remember she is not there anymore. In other moments, I unconsciously ring Merryl on my mobile phone, to ask a question that has been bothering me, and then I am jolted into recognition that she has passed away. How many nights I have turned in my bed to put my arms around Saliha only to realise that she now sleeps with the earth as her duvet. Where does one find patience for such innately natural acts?

Long-standing Western friends come and see you, put their hand on your arm, or call you, dropping the tone of their voice, to say: 'I am sorry for your loss'. The sentence is often uttered in a matter-of-fact ritualistic way, as a formality, which drains it of its meaning. At best, it expresses sympathy, suggesting they feel *for* me, as though I have a need for them to feel in a particular way. It may help if they feel *with* you. But how could they? It is an impossible ask. You appreciate their emotional intelligence. Their concern for you. They imagine it makes you feel better. It does not. Or you need some help. What help can they possibly provide? You realise, it is not sympathy you want, you want a balm for your inner turmoil. You maintain a patina of normality and graciously accept their condolences.

They say 'time heals everything'. It doesn't. Time is not a friend but an adversary of grief.

Time is dementia; it erases your memory, makes you forget, forces you to shed the segments of your life that make you a whole person. It does not ease your grief and pain. Loss of memory separates you from those you have lost. To keep their memory alive, you have to fight against time. You have to remember. You have to turn absence into presence.

To keep their memories alive, I surrounded myself with their pictures. I filled the house with photographs of Saliha. Portraits and photos of Merryl. Images of Hamida. But constantly looking at these depictions was agonising. Recollection takes its toll. It's like cancer that first slowly, then rapidly, eats away your insides. The more you remember, the more painful it gets. You feel like you are climbing a sand dune, with a camel on your back. Each step forward entrenches you deeper into the sand. You struggle to pull your foot out before taking the next step. Surrounded by the images of those you love, you try as far as possible to hide from other people.

Saliha had a friend called Shahnaz. She lived nearby so it was easy for the two friends to visit each other's house. She was a very simple person who retained the village lifestyle she had left behind in Pakistan. Always dressed in *shalwar kameez*, with a pashmina around her head and shoulders, she was much younger than Saliha, and looked up to her. She called her *baji*—elder sister. Her husband was an energetic man, with a perpetual beaming smile on his face. Then suddenly Shahnaz died. Cancer made its presence felt when it was too late and took her away within weeks. Just like Saliha. The energy and the bright smile of her husband disappeared overnight. I saw him regularly going to the local mosque, returning, and going back. I did not want to interfere in his grief. But sometimes I would stop him for a chat. He talked only about his wife because he was eager to keep her memory alive. 'I carry Shahnaz everywhere with me', he said. But remembering was devastating. He was like a tree whose roots had been cut off. The more he remembered the more he withered away. When I saw him last time, I did not recognise him. It seemed to me that he had died before his body was released from the bondage of this world. His soul had passed, but he was still breathing. His humanity had been sucked dry, but he still felt thirsty. He was not what he was, yet he existed.

I felt like him. Breathing but without the breath of life. Then on my birthday, the children gave me a card. The message inside read: 'We love you dad. We need you. Please don't die'. Something registered. Patience. Sympathy. Time. Memory. They may or may not help. You need something more to kick start again, to make sense of your remaining breaths.

You need to know. I understood that overcoming cumulative loss is like excavating a magnificent archaeological site—fresh memories on the surface, all else beneath the ground. What lies above the surface, what you and others can see, are only recent happenings. These are painful memories that trap you, surround you, and refuse to let you go. Every message of condolence is a reminder of death. But what you need to remember is life. For that you have to excavate, and carry on digging, layer by layer, till you see the whole marvellous structure below the surface. That is where you find the richness of your collective lives, discover the true splendour of love, and a modicum of solace.

This is not about what sympathisers say: 'think about the happy memories you have'. It is about self-knowledge, about knowing the depth of your relationship. My daughter said, 'Dad I never heard you say I love you to mum'. She was right. But after unearthing a few submerged memories, I understood that the need to incessantly declare one's love is for couples who require constant reassurance. Who are not mutually self-assured in their relationship. We had no such need. When Saliha and I sat on our living room sofa, to watch a Pakistani drama or listen to Coke Studio, a tranquillity swathed us. Unconditional love emanated from both of us. It was *felt* in our bodies, minds and souls. It did not have to be declared. My close friends pointed out that Merryl was always arguing and fighting with me. However, some digging made me appreciate how much I enjoyed her arguments, how many times she found faults with my reasoning, how she humanised me and how she chastised me when I was deviating from truth. When Hamida was diagnosed with dementia, relatives and friends flooded me with messages of sympathy—even empathy. But, on reflection, I know that it was precisely at that point I realised that I took my mother for granted. And I loved her even more deeply.

But truly knowing and appreciating what the departed meant to you, and how much they shaped your outlook and life, is only half of the equation. Beyond knowing, there is doing.

By knowing you begin to heal yourself. By doing you complete the process. You know that one day you will rejoin those you have lost in that numinous dimension. But before that inevitable time, you have earthly tasks to complete. Particularly the assignments the departed set themselves but were unable to finish. By working to complete these tasks you are not only doing good to their memories, you are living within them. They continue to be an integral component of your life as though they were still with you.

In my case, the tasks were obvious. Saliha did not live to retirement, to set up the charity she wanted to establish. Merryl did not live to see Anwar Ibrahim as prime minister of Malaysia and then to ensure he fulfilled all his promises. Hamida did not live to witness some of her relatives see better times. But I can fulfil these tasks: the three *khoaahish*, *tamana* and *arzoo* of my beloved. First, setting up a charity for special needs children, who Saliha loved so much, would not take much time. Although raising an endowment would. Second, looking after the extended family that Hamida was so devoted to, would require continuous long-term effort. And ensuring Malaysia, which Merryl admired so much, becomes a thriving, inclusive society and model for the Muslim world would take much longer. Love and peace and goodwill to humankind? Well, that's probably beyond my capabilities and span of life. But I will do what I can even though it may be incalculably small. Are not the oceans made of drops of water? Each step is a building block towards the continuation of the collective lives we built.

All the intellectual reasoning, and careful planning, however, does little to alleviate the pain and heal one's sorrow. I soon discovered that my heart was broken both metaphorically and physically.

A year before Saliha's death, I went for a physical check-up. One of those where they do almost every test known to modern medicine, from blood tests, stress tests, electrocardiograms, X-rays to ultrasound, CAT scans and much else besides. In Kuala Lumpur, where I was working, they do this within a day and relatively cheaply. The results were rather good. I was told that the only issue was one partly clogged artery. 'Nothing to worry about', said the consultant. 'A higher dose of statins should solve the problem'.

A year after Saliha's death, I went for the same physical examination, at my children's insistence. This time the outcome was radically different. An MRI scan revealed two arteries chock-a-block with calcium deposits. Product, the same consultant hypothesised, of 'extreme and prolonged stress'. He recommended an angiogram 'sooner rather than later'. 'Before you have a massive heart attack'. 'You need two stents', I was told.

The news did not worry me too much. But I got a tad depressed and wanted to be left alone. My daughter, Maha, thought I needed a companion to keep me company, occupied and even to feel better. A two-week-old Siamese kitten was acquired. She turned out to be an ardent explorer. We named her Tuta, after the fourteenth century Muslim traveller ibn Battuta.

The angiogram was duly performed. It revealed not two but four blocked arteries. They were fully displayed on a monitor in front of my eyes. The rather bubbly and caring consultant, a convivial man who became an instant friend, suggested that having so many stents in my body was not a good idea. There would be too much metal in my body. I could be as deadly as the local heavy metal bands. Besides, it appeared that they required a rather 'tricky and cumbersome' route to be put in their place. The best option was by-pass surgery.

A string of visitors came to see me in the hospital. One of the most notable was Wan Azizah Wan Ismail, wife of Anwar Ibrahim. Azizah personifies steadfastness and patience in the face of adversity. She has faced countless battles in her life, from decade-long struggles for her husband's release from prison, to leading a political party, to fighting numerous elections, while working as an eye surgeon, running the country as deputy prime minister, looking after her constituency as an MP and supporting her large family. Not surprisingly, she is universally admired and loved. But I adore her for another reason: she has unmatched inner calm and oozes tranquillity and spirituality in equal measure. She glided elegantly with her entourage, looked at me lying motionless in my hospital bed and shook her head in sympathy. 'Zia', she said, 'bow to the will of God. Let them go. Let them go'. She slipped a miniscule digital prayer/worry bead counter into my hand and left.

Three days later, I returned from the hospital even more depressed. But with Azizah's words echoing in my mind.

Life itself seemed to be 'tricky and cumbersome'. The only comfort: my children and close friends were around me, fussing and debating, about what I should and should not do. Stroking Tuta, who slept on an adjacent pillow by my side, was also a consolation. Every morning, precisely at 7.30, she would begin her attempts to wake me. First, she would bite my hand gently. If that did not work, she would lick my cheeks vigorously. Often, my first sight in the morning would be her big blue eyes staring back at me.

Soon afterwards, about six o'clock one morning, I found myself under the scalpel of a highly experienced and skilled surgeon, a serious, reflective man of few but precise words.

I was expecting the anaesthetist, a delightful person whose face I never saw, to ask me to count backwards from ten. Instead, she declared: 'say your prayers'. I could not but exclaim: 'shit!' I am unlikely to wake up from this sleep, I thought before I conked out.

When I woke up, some hours later, I saw dark brown eyes staring at me. I felt I was back on my own bed with Tuta gawking at me. After a few moments, I realised it was a nurse wearing rather large spectacles. She said something to me in Malay. I shook my head to say I don't understand. There was a clock on the wall right opposite my ICU bed. It read: 2 o'clock. Exactly. I tried to ask with hand movements if it was morning or evening. But the two nurses attending to me did not understand. The endotracheal tube was inserted so tight into my mouth that it was cutting through from the left side of my lips. And I found it very difficult to breathe. Unconsciously, I tried to adjust the endotracheal tube. The two nurses instantly jumped and grabbed my hands. 'No', 'No', they said in unison. Once again, I used hand signals to say I could not breath, and the tube was cutting into my cheeks. But the more I pointed to the endotracheal tube, the more agitated the nurses became. I caught a single word in their disconcerted Malay conversation: 'crazy'. Then one of them disappeared. I looked at the clock: it was still 2 o'clock. The nurse came back with two large gloves. They proceeded to put the gloves on my hands.

Fortunately, 'say your prayers' anaesthetist arrived in time. She stopped the nurses from the undesirable task. 'Are you alert?', she asked. I signalled that I needed something to write my replies on. A pad and biro were produced. I wrote: 'I am alert. But my nose is blocked'. Then pointing to the endotracheal tube, I wrote: 'Too tight, adjust'. She adjusted the tube and asked if it was loose enough for me. I nodded my head. Then, an oxygen mask was placed on my nose and mouth. It was a breath of life! I looked at the clock: still 2 o'clock.

Time had stopped. I must have been hallucinating. I was alive, but I could not stop thinking about death. I contemplated my own death. I started thinking about Epicurus, the ancient Greek philosopher, and his famous argument. Before you die, you are not yet harmed by your death. After you die, you do not exist to be harmed. So, there is no time at which you are actually harmed by death. I reflected on the death of the women I loved. What would happen if some of my close friends died? What would change? What would remain the same? After what looked like a long deliberation on morbidity and metaphysics, I was brought back to full consciousness by the bright and beaming faces of my daughter and sons, accompanied by the convivial consultant. 'Everything went according to the plan', he said. I pointed towards the clock. He turned around, had a look, and laughed. 'It stopped a long time ago! They have not bothered to change the battery'. He paused for a moment to look at his watch. 'It's 7.20 in the evening. You were in the theatre for four hours'. Then he announced that

I am expected to make a full recovery. 'You will be out of the hospital in a few days', he declared.

And so it transpired. The day after the operation, I was forced to walk with the help of a robotic machine reminiscent of the *Alien* films. Then the physios got to work. I was back in my own bed a week later. The only issue: I had to sleep on my back, which made sleeping both painful and difficult. The situation was made even more painful with Tuta jumping on my chest in her usual attempts to wake me. Three months later, my appointment with the operating consultant was very encouraging. My X-Ray looked good. Red blood cells and haemoglobin were declared wholesome. No fluid in lungs and heart just the right size. All four wires intact and sternum had healed nicely. He cut my medicines from fifteen to five pills a day. And even gave permission for me sleep on my side and the go-ahead to fly.

I returned to my abode in London after six months of enforced sojourn in Kuala Lumpur.

I saw that the front garden was totally covered with weeds, sprouting from every nook and cranny. Most of the plants in the back garden had died and withered away. Strange growths had germinated in what was left. I wept for those who made my gardens places of solace and humane dreams. After each death, I would retreat to a quiet place to sit down and mourn. Isolating myself for days. Spending most of my time listening to Munni Begum. But now her *ghazels* of separation and loss could not bring consolation to my heart. And Azizah's words—'let them go'—kept gyrating in my mind.

Then, one day, I found myself humming '*Go Sarapa Kaif-e-Ishrat Hai Sharab-e-Zindagi*'. It is the first verse from the *ghazal falsafah-e-ghaum*, or the philosophy of grief, by the great twentieth century poet and philosopher of the Indian subcontinent, Allama Muhammad Iqbal:

> Though the wine of life is the embodiment of pleasure
> The cloud of life also carries tears in its lap.
> The bubble of life dances in the wave of grief
> Alam's Surah is also part of the Book of Life.

Once read, Iqbal's poems are never forgotten. The poem is from *Bang-i-Dara*, the Call of the Marching Bell, a collection that every Pakistani child reads at secondary school. And I too read it, again and again, during my childhood. It was among the books my mother, Hamida, brought with her to London in 1961. She had me read the poems out aloud to her. Their graceful rhythm and rhyme, as well as the pure power and pleasure of the language, made them easy to memorise.

Iqbal wrote *falsafah-e-ghaum* for a friend who suffered a series of bereavements. His poems sometimes reference the Qur'an, and this one alludes to 94:5–6, from the *surah* (chapter) 'Relief'. It reads: 'Did we not relieve your heart for you and remove the burden that weighs so heavily on your back, and raise your reputation high? So surely where there is hardship there is also ease, truly where there is hardship there is also ease. So, when you are free, work on and direct your requests to your Lord'. The verse is addressed to the Prophet Muhammad, who after receiving the first revelations did not receive more for some time, did not understand what was happening to him and was overcome with grief that God had forsaken him. Iqbal generalises the verse, referred in the poem as 'Alam's Surah', and aims to provide hope not only to his friend but all his readers in their hour of need. There is also a mention of Khidr, the mythical character of Islamic literature, a being of guidance.

It's a long poem, and it ends with following lines:

> Though the dead do die they do not perish
> Really, they do not get separated from us
> When the Intellect is surrounded in worldly calamities
> Or when it is besieged in the dull night of youth
> When the heart be on the battle field of good and evil
> When journey to the goal be difficult in the darkness of
>   the road
> When the Khidr of courage be resigned from yearning
> When Intellect be helpless and conscience a silent voice
> When not a single traveller be in the vale of life
> When not even fire-fly's spark to show the way there be
> The foreheads of the dead brighten up in this darkness
> As stars are shining in the darkness of the night.

I found my mother's old, much thumbed, copy of *Bang-i-Dara* and read the poem again and again. Sometimes silently to myself. Occasionally, loudly as though reading to my mother. Slowly, the depression began to evaporate. I knew that though the three Begums had died, they did not perish. They are my Khidr, my guides. They light up the path I now take. The three Begums are not 'missing' from my life. They *are* my life.

I felt 'free', living with my grief. I had 'let go' of my three Begums—at least partially. I cleared the garden, back and front, and planted a few new plants. It was time to 'work on', I thought.

Further Reading

Hamida

For more on my relationship with my parents, see chapter one, 'Paradise Awakened', in *Desperately Seeking Paradise* (Granta, 2004); on journey to the cinema and impact of Bollywood, see 'Dilip Kumar Made Me do It', and for the mystical adventures of my Uncle Waheed, see 'My Vanishing Uncle', both in *A Person of Pakistani Origins* (Hurst, 2018).

Merryl

Merryl Wyn Davies' books are: *Knowing One Another: Shaping an Islamic Anthropology* (Mansell, London, 1988), *Darwin and Fundamentalism* (Icon Books, Cambridge, 2000) and *Introducing Anthropology* (Icon Books, Cambridge, 2000); as co-editor, with Adnan Khalil Pasha, *Beyond Frontiers: Islam and Contemporary Needs* (Mansell, London, 1989); with Ziauddin Sardar, *Faces of Islam: Conversations on Contemporary Issues* (Berita Publishing Sdn Bhd, Kuala Lumpur, 1989), *Distorted Imagination:*

Lessons from the Rushdie Affair (Grey Seal, London, 1990), *Why Do People Hate America* (Icon Books, Cambridge, 2002), *American Dream, Global Nightmare* (Icon Books, Cambridge, 2004), *Will America Change?* (Icon Books, Cambridge, 2008), *The No-Nonsense Guide to Islam* (New Internationalist, Oxford, 2004); and with Ziauddin Sardar and Ashis Nandy, *Barbaric Others: A Manifesto of Western Racism* (Pluto, London, 1993).

The citations from her works include: convert quote is from 'Living Out the Faith', *Inquiry* November 1994, p. 52; Wales quotes are from 'On the Green, Green Grass of Home' *Critical Muslim 19: Nature*, July-September 2016, pp. 241–9 and 'The Glow Linger On', *Inquiry* September 1986, p. 25; the Aberfan disaster quote is from '9/11 and All That', *Critical Muslim 2: The Idea of Islam*, April-June 2012, pp. 271–7; the rugby quote is from 'The Game's the Thing', *Inquiry* August 1986, p. 25; the BBC quotes are from 'Wink, Wink, Nudge, Nudge: This is the BBC', *Inquiry* November 1985, p. 25 and 'Programme Accidents', *Inquiry* January 1986, pp. 51–2; each month quote is from 'The Arrogance that Slew', *Inquiry* June 1986, p. 28; the Chicago Conference quote is from 'Thinking About Relevance', *Inquiry* August 1985, pp. 62–3. The Nigeria quote is from her unpublished 'Annual Community Relations Lectures', given in June 2005 at the Kensington and Chelsea Council. Her article on Pir Sabaq was published as 'The Spirit of Enterprise', *New*

Internationalist September 2011, pp. 26–7. The Indian Ocean World quote is from her unpublished work.

The many articles that Merryl Wyn Davies had in *Inquiry* include: 'The Legacy of Maududi and Shariati', *Inquiry* October 1998, pp. 34–9; 'Towards an Islamic Alternative to Western Anthropology', *Inquiry* June 1985, pp. 45–51; and 'Re-Designing a Discipline', *Inquiry* April 1986, pp. 45–9. The article on Malaysian writers, 'Writing About Malaysia', was published in September 1987, pp. 50–5.

I have described how we wrote *Distorted Imagination* and how it was eventually published, in some detail in Ziauddin Sardar, *Desperately Seeking Paradise* (Granta, London, 2004), which also contains some background on Merryl Wyn Davies. See also, Ziauddin Sardar, *The Consumption of Kuala Lumpur* (Reaktion Books, London, 2000), and Tariq Modood and Fauzia Ahmad, 'British Muslim Perspectives on Multiculturalism', *Theory, Culture & Society* 24(2), Special Issue on Global Islam, which can be downloaded from: http://www.tariqmodood.com/uploads/1/2/3/9/12392325/british_muslim_perspectives.pdf.

Saliha

To discover more about my life with Saliha, see Chapter 6, 'Bahawalnagar Wedding', of *Balti Britain: A Provocative Journey Through Asian Britain* (Granta, 2008); the Introduction to *Mecca: The Sacred City*; and the first essay in *A Person of Pakistani Origins* (Hurst, 2018).

Lazeez Khanna by Rabia Saeed was published in Lahore, 1977, in Urdu; *Quranic Advices* (mistake in the original title), Arabic Text with translation by Marmaduke Pickthall and Urdu Translation by Maulana Fateh Muhammed Jalandhari is published by Taj Company, Lahore (undated) and has been reprinted many times in many places.

Munni Begum's *ghazals* are widely available: on Spotify, Apple Music and numerous websites. *Main nazar se pi raha hun* has been sung by many artists, including Mahdi Hassan and Ghulam Ali. There is a very famous rending of *Bewafa se bhee pyaar hoita hai* by Nusrat Fateh Ali Khan. But no one can beat Munni Begum.

Poems live! But in contemporary times, the great Urdu figures who wrote the poems are often forgotten. *Main nazar se pi raha hun* was written by Anwar Mirzapuri, who flourished in Bollywood during 1960 to 1970 and wrote many memorable *ghazals* and songs. *Bewafa se bhee pyaar hoita hai* was written by Purnam Allahabadi (1940–2009). He wrote Qawwalis, including the famous *Bhar Do Jholi Meri Ya Muhammad* sung by Sabri Brothers, and songs for both Pakistani and Indian films. *Ek bar mooskura do* (which has nothing to do with the 1972 Bollywood film with the same title) was written by Kaleem Usmani (1928–2000), who worked for Radio Pakistan and the Pakistan Television Corporation. He wrote *ghazals*, poetry in praise of the Prophet Muhammad and songs for Urdu films.

The Rumi poem is from *Teachings of Rumi*, translated by E. H. Whinfield, Octagon Press, London, 1978, p. 5. The Omar Khayyam poem is from *The Rubaiyat of Omar Khayyam*, translated by Edward FitzGerald, 32 Quatrain, numerous editions.

After

Allama Muhammad Iqbal's *falsafah-e-ghaum* is poem 82 in *Bang-i-Dara*, 'The Call of the Marching Bell', translated by M. A. K. Khalil, Lahore, 1997. It is widely available on the internet. I have modified the translation a little.